S0-BDS-864

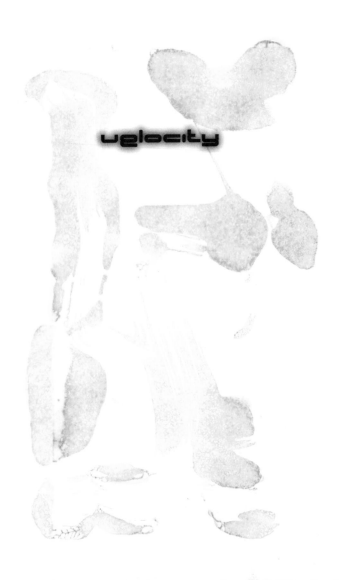

OTHER BOOKS BY SEAN DUNN

I Want the Cross!
Know Him, Serve Him

velocity

MOVING TO A SOLID FAITH

Fleming H. Revell
A Division of Baker Book House Co
Grand Rapids, Michigan 49516

© 2003 by Sean Dunn

Published by Fleming H. Revell
a division of Baker Book House Company
P.O. Box 6287, Grand Rapids, MI 49516-6287
www.bakerbooks.com

Printed in the United States of America

All rights reserved. No part of this publication may be reproduced, stored in a retrieval system, or transmitted in any form or by any means—for example, electronic, photocopy, recording—without the prior written permission of the publisher. The only exception is brief quotations in printed reviews.

Library of Congress Cataloging-in-Publication Data is on file at the Library of Congress, Washington, D.C.

Scripture quotations are from the HOLY BIBLE, NEW INTERNATIONAL VERSION®. NIV®. Copyright © 1973, 1978, 1984 by International Bible Society. Used by permission of Zondervan. All rights reserved.

contents

introduction

small stones, big falls

I must have been only eight or nine when I became enthralled with the skateboarders in the church parking lot. They were several years older than I was, and that only served to enhance my fascination with them.

Although I do not remember why my parents were at the church that afternoon, I do remember sitting and observing the antics of these teenagers the entire time. They rode with such personality. The degree of difficulty of their tricks (although nothing compared to what the pros do these days) made me watch intently with wonder in my eyes and questions in my mind. I wanted to figure out how they were doing those things.

When my dad came out of the church office and saw me with my eyes locked on the skaters, he stopped and watched with me. We talked a bit about the show that we were seeing, but nothing made me think that he was going to do what he did.

A couple of days later, my dad came home with gifts for both my brother and me. They were skateboards.

Today's boards are works of art in themselves, with their very own designers and accessories, but not boards back then. My first skateboard was an eight-inch wide piece of teal plastic with four synthetic wheels. I think it actually had flames painted on it too. Although I thought my board was cool, if I had known what boards would evolve into over the next twenty-five years, I might have been embarrassed. But compared to the skateboards that I had seen, mine was pretty nice. I was excited.

Not only was I blessed with this new board, but I had the perfect place to ride it. My house had an extended cement driveway that wrapped around the garage all the way under a parking overhang that was hidden from the road. There was plenty of open room to ride, race, and learn as many low-budget tricks as I could on my new form of transportation.

Immediately I went outside and threw my plastic with wheels on the ground. Using the built-in tail at the back, I tested my turning capabilities. Although I did not do it gracefully, I could spin and maneuver adequately enough. Now it was time to find out "what this thing could do." Starting from the carport in back, I began to pick up speed. While my right leg was pushing with all of its energy and might, my left leg balanced on the board. I picked up speed with every push. Since I was just a kid, my mind had an exaggerated sense of my velocity. I felt like I was flying along at uncontrollable speeds, yet with each push I wanted to go faster.

That's when it happened. I learned my first real lesson about skateboarding. And I learned it the hard way.

As I was flying along at breakneck speeds, my board came to an abrupt stop—but I kept going! I was sailing through the air unaccompanied by my vehicle. My expression changed instantly from one of the biggest smiles of my young life to a look of horror as I prepared for the coming impact.

After fifteen feet of flight, I landed violently on the concrete. I lost skin from my hands and knees and scraped up parts of my face and arms. I quickly went from embracing the thrill of victory to experiencing the agony of defeat. I was in pain. I was bleeding. And I was embarrassed as well.

After peeling myself off of the ground, bloody and hurt, I went in the house crying like a baby to get some consolation from my parents.

Since I was a typical young boy, my memory of the pain did not persist long enough for me to miss out on much sunlight. After a few minutes of crying and some time spent cleaning the abrasions, I had to go back outside. I wanted to master my new toy. I had to beat back my fears and vanquish my doubt. But first I had to ask a question.

What happened? What had ended my joyride and landed me face first on the cement? What had interrupted my fun and caused me so much pain? A little exploring answered my questions.

My skateboard had been conquered by an obstacle that had affected its direction, speed, and control. The nemesis was a tiny rock. Although it was barely noticeable as I skated, it had stopped my skateboard in its tracks and sent me hurtling toward the pavement. Even though I was bewildered that such a small obstacle could force me into that much chaos, I did not argue with my findings. I took care of the rock.

Then I looked around my homegrown skate park and realized that there were hundreds if not thousands of tiny rocks just like the one that had caused me grief lying in wait on the driveway. Rather than do some additional experimentation to discover just how big a rock had to be to affect my path, I chose to eliminate them all.

I went into the garage looking for answers, and I emerged with the big broom. This broom would clear a path for me. This ordinary tool would get rid of all the little fragments that were waiting for their chance to knock me down.

Five minutes with the broom and I was ready to master my board once again. I still remembered my interrupted attempt at reaching breakneck speeds, so I started slowly. However, within a few minutes I was fearlessly attacking the pavement. I owned it. The smile had returned, and I was once again enjoying the journey. Although I had been tripped up along the way, I had not been defeated. Rather than admit ruin, I had researched the obstacles, removed them, and begun enjoying the ride.

OBSTACLES ARE EVERYWHERE

I pray that as you eye the world you recognize the incredible journey that you have embarked upon. With an anticipation that both motivates and sustains you, may you make every effort to draw close to Christ and live for his purposes.

However, no matter how firmly you have decided that you are going to live with purpose and conviction, you will encounter obstacles that you must overcome. Good intentions will not be enough. You can begin with a sincere faith and build your foundation on a pure heart, but unless you survey your path, expose the obstacles, and deal with them correctly, they will make you stumble, slow down, or worse yet, fall.

Within these pages you will read about some things I learned when I wanted to live right but sometimes got caught off guard by unseen obstacles. You will look into the lives of other teenagers who have experienced hurdles. Some of them adjusted correctly and overcame, while others are still reeling from their effects.

You will hear warning signals in this book. I believe that you will also find encouragement and discover some practical truths that will help you become the stable, steady, passionate, and on-target Christian that you want to be.

WHERE WE'RE GOING

Each of the chapters in this book will highlight a specific area that commonly leads to the disruption of many Christian young people's faith walks. They have led to the downfall of many in your generation as well as many who have come before you.

From my observations, research, conversations with young people, and personal experiences, I have found that many of the obstacles that tend to make teenagers stumble can be classified in four categories:

Entertainment
Relationships
Image
Emotions

Many people who have not taken the dangers in these four areas seriously have struggled to live victoriously in their faith.

One of the difficulties of writing about these topics is trying to do it in a way that will not make readers defensive. Some of these topics are sensitive and have caused tension between people, and especially between different generations, for decades. Opinions and preferences have been so strong that some people have had difficulty even listening to someone who disagrees with them—let alone really hearing them.

So I ask you to read with an open heart and mind. Don't listen for the opinion of the author, but for the thoughts of your heavenly Father. I will not try to influence you with my personal feelings and my "old-guy" mentality, but I will strive to communicate the principles of Scripture and the foundations on which to build a godly life. You have my permission to disagree with me, but if you ignore God as he tries to speak to you and direct you, your faith will suffer.

Although the discussion of many of these issues has been either ignored or sugarcoated, their influence, origin, and impact must be evaluated, exposed, and attacked. It is time to sweep the pavement and make a clear path. It is time for the memories of the falls to be put in the past. Your journey is too precious to be continually interrupted by little obstacles. It's time to get moving.

Are you ready?

PERSONAL GAME PLAN

Ask Yourself This—As you begin this book, do you realize that to avoid the obstacles that will try to impede your spiritual growth you will have to make some decisions that are both difficult and unpopular? Are you willing to listen to God's voice and obey his direction, no matter how difficult?

Key Scripture—"Search me, O God, and know my heart; test me and know my anxious thoughts. See if there is any offensive way in me, and lead me in the way everlasting." Psalm 139:23–24

Ask God to Help—If you truly want God to help you recognize and avoid the obstacles in your life, you need to come to him humbly. You can begin by praying this prayer from your heart, *"Lord, I love you more than anything else in this world, and I want nothing more than to walk closely with you. I pray that* *you would open my eyes to the dangers that lie before me so that I can avoid them. I also pray that you would allow me to hear your voice speaking to me and that I would be willing to obey you no matter what the cost. I ask these things in Jesus' name. Amen."*

entertainment

1

hollywood disciples

I grew up in a Christian home where I learned about morality and purity. For the most part those things were modeled for me and even though they were not regular topics of discussion, I knew what was right from what was wrong.

At an early age, I knew that I wanted to be a godly man who would treat others properly and help them become better people. I wanted my life to count and tried to be a positive influence on those closest to me.

My spiritual life was developing, and although there were areas of struggle, I was trying to walk in submission to God's will for my life. I was serving in many areas of ministry. My friends knew me as someone with convictions that came from my faith in God. And for the most part, I was full of joy and a good friend.

However, although I was doing a decent job of being a good example of Christianity, I had a couple of chinks in my armor. While Christ was trying to develop in me the character that would make my calling possible, the devil and society in general were trying to ruin my character. One of the main things that I was dealing with was my thought life.

I was working hard to see my mind renewed (see Romans 12:2) and to focus on things that were pure in nature (see Philippians 4:8), but I was still in a war. The sexual thoughts that were embedded in my mind were dominating my life. I knew that God had called me to be pure and to have a holy thought life, but I seemed to be losing that battle. It was a frustrating struggle.

Around age sixteen, after having fought this fight for at least two years, I began to observe what things influenced me in these ways. I thought of friends at school who were constantly talking about girls and making sexual jokes. I recalled the times that my eyes had been drawn to a girl who was wearing something provocative. I remembered the times that I had been captivated by an ad in a store window or on a billboard flaunting a female's body. I also thought about the commercials and television shows I had recently seen that were putting impure thoughts in my mind.

Almost everywhere I looked, sexual things were demanding my attention. I could find nowhere to go to totally escape from the images that had been strategically placed in my view and constantly fed my immoral thought life. Even when I tried to avoid them, they were present.

As I began to pray and beg God to renew my mind and work in my thought life, I realized that there were some actions I could take to protect myself. The first thing I thought of was the movies that I watched.

Although I wanted to be pure, one side of me was intrigued by the same things that disgusted me. The spirit side of me knew that the obsession I had developed with the female body was wrong, but my flesh liked it. As much as I hated thinking the thoughts, I was drawn to the images that produced them. Nowhere was this as evident as in my movie choices.

I grew up thirteen miles outside of Spokane, Washington. The separation from civilization meant that I was often home alone after school and during the summers. Without much to do and with few friends nearby, I would regularly walk down to the local convenience store to rent a movie or two to occupy the time.

Over the course of time, I developed a habit of choosing my movies based on the cover, not on the content. I wasn't obsessed with entertainment; I was being seduced by skin. If the cover of the movie had a cute woman clad in less than adequate clothing, I would rent it and sneak it into the house.

I began to realize that these movies were tearing me away from what I said I wanted to be. I had to make a conscious choice. Weighing the options and deciding that my character and spiritual life meant more to me than the things that I had let tempt me, I chose to monitor the movies I would see. That summer I decided that I would not watch R-rated movies and I would get the scoop on the PG-13 movies that interested me before I would go see them. At all costs, I would avoid sexual content. I decided that I couldn't protect myself from all forms of visual stimuli, but I could protect myself in the area of my movies—and therefore I had to.

Three young men stopped by my office on a Thursday afternoon. School was out and they were getting ready to go see a movie. As soon as I asked which one, I could tell that they did not want to tell me. After a few attempts to avoid the subject, one of the guys told me straight out. As soon as I heard the title, I knew the movie. The newspaper had made a commotion about it because the content was too steamy for even an R rating. The movie had been released the week before with an NC-17 rating.

I could tell that they were embarrassed, but I pushed the conversation further. "Why would you go see that?" I asked. One answered slyly, "I am supposed to do a movie review for the school paper." After a few minutes of debate about whether they should go see this movie, which was laced with sexual content and naked females, I told them, "The only reason you are going to see it is to see the flesh."

Although they did not want to admit it, they could not deny that my observation was correct. These young men, who wanted to grow up and be godly men, were making a poor choice that day. They said they wanted to be virgins when they got married, but their choices were stealing their purity and polluting their innocence.

Four eighth grade girls were talking about the latest movie before the youth service. I told them that they shouldn't go see that particular movie. "Why?" one asked, with a defensive tone in her voice. I told her, "Listen, I have seen the trailers and it is not a good movie. It is about the occult."

One seemed to be listening, but the others had already made up their minds, and nothing I said that night was going to change that.

The next morning as I was praying, I felt like the Lord wanted me to go see the movie so I could share with these young ladies why they should avoid it. Although I tried to talk God out of it (I do like movies, but dark movies about the occult that are targeted at a female teenage audience don't excite me), I realized that I had better obey him. That afternoon I talked to every one of the pastors at the church, and no one was willing to go with me. My pastor said, "I'm glad you are going so that you can talk about it intelligently, but it looks creepy to me. I'm not going." (Note: This is the only movie that I ever went to see for this reason. God did not need me to go to the movie rated NC-17 for sexual content so that I could speak wisely about that one!)

So off to the theater I headed all alone. I got there five minutes before it started and watched the people filter into the room. One by one, a dark crowd snuck in, many of them wearing clothes and symbols that implied they were involved in witchcraft and occult practices.

The atmosphere was creepy. The room definitely had a demonic feel. When the movie started, it got worse. I sat there for over an hour and a half with my skin crawling. I wanted to leave after the first scene, but knew that I had to stay. I received quite the education.

On Sunday, I quickly walked up to the girls that had been talking about the movie and asked if they had seen it yet. They had not. I gave them a brief review. "The movie is trying to teach people your age how to get involved in witchcraft. It shows you where to get books on witchcraft, how to cast a few spells, and how to play a few spiritual games. It is a recruitment tool and a how-to movie. Please don't go." They decided not to go.

This movie would have been an unwise choice for these girls. Knowing them, I have a sense that one or more of them might have been caught up by the movie enough to try some of the things that they saw.

A young man was talking about the latest movie after church. He was telling one of his friends how funny it was. "You have to go see it. It's hilarious!"

The problem is that I know the guy who did see it, and I know that he struggles with his thought life. The movie that he was going on about was dubbed by the media as a very funny movie, but the commercials alone were on the verge of being rated R. The advertisements tied in a few provocative images to get guys like him interested, and I am sure that once he was in the theater, he was bombarded with images of flesh.

He made a poor choice. Although I knew from previous conversations with him about his thought life that he was absolutely frustrated with his weakness, he decided that for one evening laughing was more important than being pure. The movie choice he made was fighting against him.

One of our college-aged youth leaders skipped a meeting one night because he was at a movie. A couple of days later I bumped into his mom, who apologized for him. Not knowing anything about the movie itself, she inadvertently volunteered the name of the movie he had seen that night. I didn't say anything to her, but I thought to myself that he had not acted wisely.

The movie that he had viewed was not the worst in the world. It was not sexual in nature, but it was built around a theme that Christians should not support with their money or risk viewing. The movie was an "action" movie about the devil coming out of hell to get a bride. A week later, I had the opportunity to talk to the leader about my concerns. As I expected, he defended his choice by pointing out the one good point in the movie. From what I understand, good wins over evil in the end, but movies like that always give more credibility to Satan than he deserves.

You might think that I am being a little too old fashioned about this movie, but I disagree. If Christians want Hollywood to adopt a more moral stance, we must prove it by not paying out our money when they put out trash. And I don't believe that anyone who is trying to walk with God should take a chance of being influenced by these horrific plots, themes, and philosophies.

KNOW YOUR COMPETITION

Many students stumble over entertainment choices. Hollywood seems determined to "disciple" the younger generation with its own moral stances, attitudes, and opinions. However, most of those things contradict what God would have for us. You must make wise choices about entertainment or you will be vulnerable.

I am very aware that some people will read this chapter with their defenses up. Some are waiting for me to give them a legalistic rule for what they can and cannot watch so they can disagree, get angry, and decide to ignore the rest of this book.

I am not here to give you a list of movies and actors and tell you whether or not you should invest time and money in them. I am here, however, to give you the principles that I believe should be applied to your entertainment choices.

You should not be seeking my opinion, but God's. My prayer is that as you read you will allow God to help you evaluate your entertainment based on your spiritual intent. If you declare with your mouth that you want to be godly and to protect your innocence, then you must show it with your actions. If you say that you want to be holy and set apart for

God to use, then you must be careful what you ingest into your life.

LEARN GOD'S APPROACH

Although the Bible does not speak directly about movies, entertainment, or Hollywood, several scriptural principles apply. Here are a few Scriptures to help you make intelligent decisions about entertainment.

> Flee the evil desires of youth, and pursue righteousness, faith, love and peace, along with those who call on the Lord out of a pure heart.
>
> 2 Timothy 2:22

> Above all else, guard your heart, for it is the wellspring of life.
>
> Proverbs 4:23

> See to it that no one takes you captive through hollow and deceptive philosophy, which depends on human tradition and the basic principles of this world rather than on Christ.
>
> Colossians 2:8

TAKE THE CHALLENGE

Movies today are filled with things that can be destructive to a Christian's resolve and convictions. You would be wise to know yourself and recognize your weaknesses so that you can protect yourself. Whatever your personal weaknesses are, every Christian should work to avoid overdoses of certain things.

Sexual content. Although our society is saturated with sexual images, innuendo, and conversation, people who want to be strong in their convictions must filter their intake as much as possible. You should not only be aware of what is excess for you, but also work with the people that you spend time with so you can protect each other. Even if you think that you have a handle on your mind and do not struggle with sexual thoughts, one of your friends might struggle and not be good at protecting himself. When you hang around him, you can help him be a stronger person simply by avoiding certain movies.

Negative and cynical views of God. Our world does not always refer to our Lord kindly, so I am not surprised that Hollywood struggles to present a positive view of God or people who are trying to serve him. However, when moviemakers go out of their way to spread an image of God that is offensive to him, our hearts should be offended as well. Do not volunteer to sit for two hours in front of actors who are mocking the person and the values that you should be basing your life around.

Violence and anger. Many people have personal struggles in these areas, yet continually feed on entertainment that shows people acting on their intense emotions instead of dealing with them in a positive manner. If you struggle to control your anger, you should avoid certain movies. Although you may think it is "just a harmless action flick," if it is feeding outbursts of emotion that you are not yet in control of, you would be better off saving your money.

Occult movies. Although your mind may be able to distinguish between reality and fiction, you do not have any good reason to sit through a production that tries to convince you that supernatural forces other than God should be either embraced or feared. As a Christian, you already worship and walk in relationship with the most powerful supernatural influence the world can ever know. But many people are seduced away into a world of "harmless" occult practices because they let down their defenses and become fixated on things that God does not want them to become familiar with. As they innocently gaze at these things, their curiosity draws them into dangerous places.

Have you ever sat through a movie that made you cringe with disgust? Have you ever seen something on the screen that you wished you could erase from your memory?

What about this: Have you ever walked out of a movie? Have you ever refused to watch a movie at a friend's house because you knew the content was inappropriate?

In today's society you must know your convictions and live by them. You must know what kind of movies will begin to tear away at the person that you want to be, and you must be willing to avoid them.

If you are going to not trip on this hurdle, you must be willing to stay home when your group of friends is heading to the theater to see a movie that you know will force some immoral or negative things down your throat. At the cost of some embarrassment, you must be willing to get up and walk out of a movie that catches you off guard. If your friends are watching something that you can't comfortably sit through and you can't talk them into another activity, you need to go into another room. Your spiritual life is more important than not seeing the latest movie and more important than the reactions you might receive from your friends.

Having a desire to be godly is one thing; having thought through your convictions and boundaries is another. Don't let movies make you stumble, and don't let Hollywood disciple you into ungodly ways of thinking and living.

PERSONAL GAME PLAN

Ask Yourself This—Do you believe that the entertainment choices you have made in the past have helped shape your philosophies of life? Have you been influenced in a positive or negative way? Do any changes need to take place in this area of your life if you are going to walk closely with God?

Key Scripture—"See to it that no one takes you captive through hollow and deceptive philosophy, which depends on human tradition and the basic principles of this world rather than on Christ." Colossians 2:8

Ask God to Help—Pray for the strength to choose your entertainment wisely. *"God, help me to make wise choices that protect me when it comes to my entertainment choices. I want to think about life, love, and the world the way that you do. May your attitudes be mine and may my thoughts be pure. Amen."*

2

Disciples
or groupies?

I was standing on the third floor hallway in the Mall of America when I heard some music. Curious, I listened, and when I sensed the direction, I followed the sound to see what was happening.

Looking down over a balcony, I saw a crowd of people in front of a stage occupied by a female singer and two dancers. I asked another onlooker who was performing. Although this woman knew the name of the musical artist, I had never heard of her before. (Because I want to talk about principles and not specific people you may have opinions about, I am not going to mention her name. However, since that time, I have watched this artist on some interviews and have reviewed her lyrics. I now have a pretty clear picture of her message and her influence.) From where I was standing, I could not get the full experience of the concert, but I did begin to analyze what I was seeing.

As a minister who works with young people, I try to pay attention to what influence the media has in their lives. One way I evaluate all forms of entertainment and media is by asking two questions:

1. What is the target audience? Looking down from my perch, I observed the people standing in front of the stage. Several hundred had gathered there, but there were primarily two groups represented: girls between the ages of ten and sixteen, and guys averaging around sixteen years old. The girls were there because they liked the music. The guys were there

because they liked the singer. She was dressed provocatively and achieving her goal of getting attention with her body.

Because her target audience was the age bracket that I continually work
with, I paid special attention to the second question.

2. What message are they trying to communicate? Because the speak-
ers were pointed directly at the audience and I was almost directly above
the stage, I was unable to understand the majority of the lyrics to the
songs. However, on the last song of the set, I could completely understand
the content of the chorus.

Although it was not the most sexually explicit song that I have ever
heard, what I heard and saw did disturb me. It was feeding our society's
philosophy that young people need to be sexually aware and flirtatious.
The song was explicitly sharing that message and the dance moves were
backing it up. Not only was the performer rubbing her body, but all of the
ten-year-old girls were as well.

Some might argue that the song was "not that bad," and I might agree.
However, I believe that any medium that tries to teach our females in their
pre-teen years that they should relate to all males on a sexual level and
use their bodies to manipulate and tease the people around them is wrong.

That experience made quite an impact on me. It reopened my eyes to
the influence that the music industry has on teens and pre-teens. As I was
looking at the crowd, I wondered how many of the young ladies who were
imitating the singer were from Christian homes. I thought about the young
men who were trying to stay pure in the way that they thought about the
females around them yet were continually teased and enticed by the stars
of the pop scene.

KNOW YOUR COMPETITION

As I travel and preach the message of Christ, I find that music
is one of the main things that I am competing against for the
attention of teenagers. Although I love music and believe that
God has used it to bless my life in tremendous ways over the
years, I do not want to overlook the fact that music can create
obstacles for Christians who put too much emphasis on it. In
this chapter, I want to attempt to bring a balance. My goal is
to present principles that are timeless and true. Then you will

be able to decide how to apply these standards to how music influences your life. Here are some of the negative things that music can produce in the lives of even the most well-intentioned Christians.

Music can produce negative attitudes. Just as good music can produce godly thoughts, worldly music can suggest wrong ideas which, when continually fed into your mind, can produce negative attitudes. Some music promotes anger. Some people applaud hostility and rebellion, but these things in turn will lead to hatred. These are not appropriate attitudes for Christians to have festering in our lives. We want to be people who love the Lord, love other people, submit to authority, and live honorable lives. Some of the musical influences that we readily ingest fight against these goals.

Music can feed fleshly desires that we are trying to crucify. Although many teenagers are trying to put to death the evil desires of their flesh that wage war against their souls, some music that they choose feeds those desires. Quite a bit of today's music feeds the lust that we are trying to flee. The lyrics, the lifestyles, and the visual images that create the music culture are sexual in nature. Instead of love songs, people are writing lust songs. Rather than singing about what their hearts love, they are singing about what their bodies want. Don't think that you can become absorbed in this music and not be influenced by it.

Music can be a distraction. Even those who are able to avoid the sinful pitfalls that snag so many people can be distracted by music. Instead of focusing their attention on Christ and spending regular time getting to know him, some people get so caught up in music that they neglect the things that really matter. Instead of reserving a place to meet with God, they fill their bedrooms with music all of the time. Enjoying music is not sin, but it can keep you from your goal of knowing Christ.

Music preaches a message and can slowly lead even Christians astray. I have the privilege of traveling and preaching the message of Christ all over the world. In the same way, musicians cut CDs and go on tours sharing their philosophies. Sometimes they push specific agendas, while at other times the attitudes that affect the way they live their lives are unintentionally presented. Sometimes the messages are subtle and have to be looked for to be seen. However, some musicians are abrasive and aggressive in their appeal. Whether you are willing to admit it or not, music does affect the way that you think about life. If you have a steady diet of vain or destructive philosophies, your convictions will be affected and your philosophy of life will be altered.

Learn God's Approach

I love music. It has been a beneficial and uplifting thing in my life. Here are some of the great things that music can do for a person.

Music can help people worship. Worship music has really helped me to connect with God. Whether in church, my car, my office, or my home, I can listen to certain music and be drawn into God's presence. Music has definitely strengthened my bond with Christ. The Bible also directs us to worship God through music, as seen in Psalm 150: "Praise the LORD. Praise God in his sanctuary; praise him in his mighty heavens. Praise him for his acts of power; praise him for his surpassing greatness. Praise him with the sounding of the trumpet, praise him with the harp and lyre, praise him with tambourine and dancing, praise him with the strings and flute, praise him with the clash of cymbals, praise him with resounding cymbals. Let everything that has breath praise the LORD. Praise the LORD."

Music can be an encouragement. At difficult times in my life and on difficult days, a good song or quality CD has often helped me feel like I could go on. Some songs help me have a better perspective on life. Songs have proven to be a source of encouragement to me at times. Music can help us remember the good things God has done, as seen in Psalm 98:1: "Sing to the LORD a new song, for he has done marvelous things; his right hand and his holy arm have worked salvation for him."

Music can help people relax. Some people use music as a tool to help them forget about the tension of the day. It helps them escape their anxious thoughts and pressing responsibilities. Music can help you emotionally and mentally break away. First Samuel 16:23 says, "Whenever the spirit from God came upon Saul, David would take his harp and play. Then relief would come to Saul; he would feel better, and the evil spirit would leave him."

Music can help you change your mood. At times I have been tired, but by carefully choosing an appropriate song, I have found energy that I did not know I had left in my body. Music can enhance any mood, whether thoughtful, playful, or joyful. As Psalm 45:8 says, "the music of the strings makes you glad."

TAKE THE CHALLENGE

I am sure you would agree that music offers too many positives to be avoided because of the negative possibilities. Very few people are willing to dismiss music as a form of entertainment. So instead of trying to convince you that you should stay away altogether, I am going to suggest a few principles that will help you enjoy it without letting it keep you away from your goals.

Keep your priorities straight. Many people are unwilling to evaluate the things that they have been enjoying over the years because they would rather hold onto their rights and protect their preferences. However, if you are going to be wise, you need to keep your relationship with Christ and your spiritual development as your number one priority. If you are able to do this, you will not be afraid to examine your music choices and let God speak to you about them. But if your priorities are slightly out of line, you will not allow God to direct you. Seeing the big picture of what you are trying to do and to become will make the difficult decisions that much easier. When you realize that music affects your overall direction and goals, you will not find it as difficult to obey God in these areas.

Ask God for his direction. You will easily find people who have strong opinions on these areas of entertainment. However, you are not looking for man's ideas, but God's. If you ask him for wisdom, he will give it to you. The key is obedience. When God speaks to you about your actions, you are obligated to obey. That is why many people never ask God to direct them in these areas.

Don't live by someone else's convictions, and don't try to make anyone else live by yours. Of course some exceptions apply to this rule. If the convictions being stated by someone are taken directly from the Word of God, they are absolutes and should apply to everyone. But if they are personal convictions spoken specifically to an individual's heart by God, you are not held accountable for that command.

Another situation in which you must obey someone else's request is in obeying your parents. If your parents say you cannot listen to any secular music or to a certain group, you are obligated by Scripture to obey them, even if you don't agree or don't want to obey. To disobey your parents' direct orders is a sin.

Weed out the negative influences in your music. As you prayerfully look at your music choices, you may find some groups or singers that are not the best influences. Even if it takes going to your journal and specifically writing down "God told me to stop listening to _____," you should weed them out of your selections. You are better off being too cautious on the side of purity than continuing to feed your mind and heart these influences.

Listen to a steady diet of worship music. As I travel, I am seeing stronger Christians at a younger age than I ever have before. One thing that is consistently true about young people who are maturing earlier and standing stronger is that they love worship and spend a good amount of time connecting with God through worship and praise music. Worship music, no matter what style, helps you focus on Christ. It forces you to look beyond your own circumstances and get past the petty things that fight for your attention so you can concentrate on the one who truly is worthy. When you worship, your faith is strengthened. If you regularly include worship in your life, you will become stronger in your walk with God.

OVERCOME THE OBSTACLES

Not too long ago I walked into a youth room in a local church where no one knew I was that night's preacher. With a cover of anonymity that I rarely enjoy, I walked around the room listening to conversations.

Standing against one wall were a couple of teens. Evidently one was a guest of someone who regularly attended the youth group. He quickly told the group that he didn't understand how a "God of love" could let terrible things happen in the world. Trying to get a reaction from the Christians there, he went on to say that God must have a cruel sense of humor.

I watched in amazement as none of the Christian young people said a word. They stood there confused and scared.

I watched the group for several minutes. As they moved past the first topic of discussion, the young man pointed out a T-shirt with the name of a Christian band on it. "I went to their concert. They blow!"

With that comment he brought down the anger of three of the young people. They spoke up to defend that band like it was their sworn duty before God himself.

Shaking my head, I left the room realizing that we are more often groupies than disciples. For years I have observed how teenagers would rather defend their favorite music groups than their faith. If you attack their God they will turn the other cheek, but if you insult their bands, they will go to war. Many Christian young people have become so obsessed with their music that they have begun to worship the musicians. They have lost all perspective on their music and faith.

I pray that more people would rise up in the name of Christ than in the name of the newest group. We need more disciples and fewer groupies. Which one are you?

PERSONAL GAME PLAN

Ask Yourself This—Is music an obstacle in your life that slows down your spiritual pursuit and weakens your convictions? Do certain things you listen to plant seeds of anger or immorality in your mind? Do you have an unhealthy attraction to the musicians that you respect?

Key Scripture—"Finally, brothers, whatever is true, whatever is noble, whatever is right, whatever is pure, whatever is lovely, whatever is admirable—if anything is excellent or praiseworthy—think about such things." Philippians 4:8

Ask God to Help—Pray that music does not become an obsession and an idol to you as it has to so many. *"God, although I want to enjoy everything that you have chosen to bless me with, I do not want to have any idols in my life. May music never be an idol. Lord, I give up my right to choose the music I listen to, and I ask you for your wisdom. Teach me to worship you in spirit and in truth and to avoid being tripped up by this obstacle in life. Amen."*

3

addicted to activity

Taylor told me, "I just don't have time." I have heard this from many students, yet every time the subject comes up I am amazed. This time I heard the excuse from Taylor, who had come up to talk with me just after I finished speaking at a youth convention on the benefits of spending time with God. He had agreed with everything that I said during the service, but his conviction was overpowered by the lie he had bought.

We sat down for a quick conversation. "So, you don't have any time to spend with God?" He replied, "I don't. I mean, with school, sports, and church, I barely have enough time to get my homework done."

Not wanting to offend him but wanting more information, I asked a couple of questions. "Do you watch TV?" "Some, but not much," he said. I asked, "How much did you watch last week?" After he realized that I was serious, he began to think. After a brief pause, he replied, "Maybe six or seven hours."

After a series of questions, I began to see what was happening with this young man. I realized that although he was not letting one single thing dominate his time, many things were nipping away at it. He invested his time in many different things over the course of the average week. Some would be spent running around with friends, some playing video games, some watching TV, some on the Internet, and some more on the phone. Even though he said he did not have enough time in a week to invest in his spiritual life, he seemed to have time to do everything else.

He said that he was frustrated because he had too much to do and not enough time to do it, but I made another observation. "I think you are addicted to activity. I think your time has slipped away from you because you always have something to do, someone to be with, or somewhere to go."

He sat there for a moment just looking at me. As my words sunk in, he looked at the ground. "I guess you're right. I'm always doing something or looking for the next activity."

KNOW YOUR COMPETITION

Although I realize that society pushes everyone, including teenagers, into living at a hectic and exhausting pace, I don't believe that we are to be slaves to our schedules. Rather, our routines should allow us to include everything that we truly find important.

As a young person who wants to mature into a man or woman of God who has a tremendous impact on the world, you must take time out of your schedule to invest in your spiritual life and build on your godly foundations. If you ignore your relationship with God, you will begin to lose your passion for God. A neglected faith will become weak, shallow, and boring. However, if you carve out time to strengthen your faith through spending time with God in quiet places, you will be on the road to maturity.

One of the main reasons that people in our society neglect their spiritual development and growth is that they are over-occupied. They have become addicted to activity.

People who are addicted to activity don't feel that they have enough time to do the most important things in their life. Their schedules control them and work against their stated goals. When people get caught in the endless maze of events and happenings that are offered and encouraged by society, they neglect what is most precious to them.

Learn God's Approach

Scripture makes it clear that God wants us to walk closely with him. Like in any relationship, that takes effort. God wants our main focus to be on him. When God is most important, the rest of the world comes into balance and perspective. His Word teaches:

> But seek first his kingdom and his righteousness, and all these things will be given to you as well.
>
> Matthew 6:33

> Delight yourself in the LORD and he will give you the desires of your heart.
>
> Psalm 37:4

> But his delight is in the law of the LORD, and on his law he meditates day and night.
>
> Psalm 1:2

God commands us to seek him, delight ourselves in him, and meditate on his Word. That is his number one goal for our lives as we begin to build a relationship with him. If we become so busy with other activities that we are left with no time to pursue God, we have made a mistake somewhere along the way.

Take the Challenge

If you recognize that you tend to be addicted to activity, you might need to make some minor adjustments. If you realize that you have neglected God because your time continually slips away from you, something must be done. Here are a few suggestions.

You must prioritize God. Although many people think getting to know God is a good idea, most do not make God a priority. So each day slips away without any activity that will bring spiritual growth. Rather than waiting for a convenient time to spend time with God, you must make him a priority. Set a regular time and stick to it. Don't let anything interfere with your time alone with God.

Try to schedule your time with God for the time when you are most in control. For me that is in the morning. Although I always know when I need to leave the house to start my day, I rarely know what I will be doing in the evening. So I choose to spend time with God in the morning. By simply setting my alarm clock, I can carve out time with God in a part of my day that has few surprises. Whatever time of day you choose, make sure that you find a routine that works for you. Don't leave it to chance. Make it a priority and stick to it.

Evaluate the time wasters in your life. When I talked to Taylor as I described at the beginning of this chapter, we began to list the activities that often stole his time. He realized that he lost time in several areas of his life by simply getting caught up in what he was doing. He might mean to play just one game of solitaire on the computer, but he would waste an hour there. Sometimes it was the phone. He would pick it up to ask his girlfriend a quick question about school, but by the time he hung up the phone he had given her a large chunk of time.

What I recommended to him and what I advise you to do is this: Evaluate yourself for a week. Recognize the things in your life that tend to take up your time. At the same time, evaluate the unspoken goals you have for your life. Then compare them to find the things that steal your time but aren't that important in the big picture of your life.

If you do not discover the things that are stealing your time, you are silently giving them permission to continue to steal from you. But if you recognize them, you can begin to take back control of your time.

Avoid things that will capture you and waste your time. I recently stayed with my mom while on a trip. I was speaking at a Christian school in the area in the mornings and had a couple of evening meetings set up as well. On Wednesday I had a couple of hours off, and I had good intentions of doing two things. I needed to finish preparing for my evening message, and I was in desperate need of a nap.

As I drove back to my mom's, I was really looking forward to my afternoon. I had it all planned out. The first thing that I was going to do was sleep. After that I was going to get ready for the youth group meeting that night. When I arrived I grabbed a snack and sat on the couch. I picked up the remote control for the television. This proved to be my mistake.

For two and one-half hours I sat there flipping through the channels, looking for something worth watching. Although I never spent more than fifteen minutes on any one station, I wasted a large chunk of time. Before I knew what had happened, I looked at the clock and realized that the day had slipped away and I needed to get ready for my meeting.

Frustrated with myself, I changed clothes and took a few minutes to pray. I never did get my nap. And although I had a great opportunity to invest in my love relationship with Christ, I missed it because I got caught up in something far less important.

Although the remote control was not a sin, I should have avoided it. I know that I tend to get seduced into an unproductive trance by the television, but I thought I could limit my time. Well, I proved to myself that I couldn't.

Just as you should avoid the things that draw you into sin, you should avoid the things that keep you from spending time with God. If you tend to get caught up in video games, don't play a game if you haven't taken time for God. Is your weakness television? Don't indulge until you have had your quiet time. When you go out with your friends, do you seem to lose track of time and waste the entire day when you only planned to be out for a short time? If so, make sure that you spend time with God before you go out.

Stop using excuses. If you have ever argued that you "just don't have time" for God, you must realize that this is an excuse and stop using it. You have just as much time in each of your days as everyone else in the world—the only question is, what are you going to do with it? Are you going to invest it wisely in your spiritual development, or are you going to let it slip away from you?

No excuse can cover the truth. If you are addicted to being busy and other activities mean more to you than spending time with God, just begin to admit it. Your priorities can be seen in how you spend your time, so learn to be truthful with yourself. If you don't like the conclusions that you are forced to make, maybe you need to change your priorities.

OVERCOME THE OBSTACLES

What an encouraging e-mail. I had met Stephanie at a camp that I had spoken at. Her message told me she was remembering what she had learned.

"Since camp, I have been spending time with God every day. At first I thought I would just start with fifteen minutes a day, but I can't get enough. Some days I am up until two or three in the morning just reading the Bible and talking to God. I just can't seem to get enough!"

Stephanie went on to tell me how several areas of her life were being affected by her newfound desire to get close to God. But she also told me about the things she had to give up. In her note she told me that she had to give up some of her television shows and music so that she had time for God. That was hard at first, but she did not notice it anymore. God was meeting her in such a special way that the activities that had dominated her life were barely missed.

I have to admit I am proud of Stephanie.

If you want to grow with God, don't trip on the obstacles that can steal your time. Make sure that you carve out time to spend with God. You won't regret it!

personal game plan

Ask Yourself This—Are you addicted to activity? What are some of the things that tend to steal your time? Do you spend time with God on a regular basis? Are you going to begin to make those times a priority? When are you going to set up your appointment?

Key Scripture—"But seek first his kingdom and his righteousness, and all these things will be given to you as well." Matthew 6:33

Ask God to Help—Pray that God would help you make him a priority in how you use your time. *"Lord Jesus, I realize that you should be my first priority. Would you help me with that?*

I confess my tendency to waste time and leave little for you. Please help me avoid the things that steal my time. Give me a greater desire to know you. God, as I set aside time for you, please meet me. May your Word come alive to me and may I feel your presence. I love you and I want to grow in my faith. Amen."

relationships

4

who's number one?

Rich was a great guy. Everyone in the church liked him. His parents had raised him to be a moral young man who made proper decisions in most areas of life. Although he was far from perfect, he was definitely conscientious and caring. He did not act carelessly but thought through how his decisions and actions would affect others.

Spiritually, Rich was solid. At a young age he began doing missions work in the summer and serving in many areas of the church throughout the year. Connecting with God was his ambition and serving God was his goal. Rich was not perfect in this area either, but he was consistently and aggressively seeking God and wanting to become more like him.

Rich was a model Christian and an example to many.

But his life began to subtly change direction when he started dating an older girl. Although Karen was mature for her age and a Christian, she became a distraction to him. The change did not take place overnight, but after several months, his passion for Christ was noticeably different. Rather than show up to church early with the desire to serve, he would show up late and leave early—always with Karen, his newfound love. Whereas previously he had been open about his spiritual life, both his successes and struggles, he began to hide and become defensive when concern was shown.

Although I cared deeply about Rich and wanted to see him succeed in life, I saw him slip away from his spiritual goals. His relationship with Karen became an obstacle to him that led to struggles in his faith and convictions. His priorities became distorted and his spiritual life was affected in dramatic ways.

Lisa was a typical girl who grew up in a churchgoing family. Sweet disposition, friendly smile, and a loving heart. She had advantages that many other young people who were in my youth group did not have. Her parents loved her and loved the Lord. They were not rich, but they provided nicely for her needs and graciously gave her many of her desires. She was encouraged to attend church regularly, but not forced. Her parents made their family's faith something to be shared as they tried to raise their children in an environment that would encourage spiritual growth.

So how did Lisa end up so far away from the Lord?

I first met Lisa when she was thirteen. Her family had just moved into our area and begun coming to our church. She enthusiastically told me that she couldn't wait to get involved and wanted to not only be a part of what was going on, but also serve anywhere and in any way that she could. She was excited about the opportunities that our group would offer her for social outlets and spiritual development.

However, by the time she was fifteen, her spiritual goals had been put on the shelf. Instead of pursuing God as her number one priority, Lisa began to place a higher priority on her friends. Although she might have done well if the friends who influenced her had been from the church, the opposite was true. Because she did not find instant companionship within our church, she hooked up with the rebellious group from her junior high. Lisa began to take on their attitudes and soon to mimic their actions. Before too long she was sharing their addictions.

Her faith was something that she would visit on occasion, but nothing that she could sustain. Her priority of finding relationships and keeping them came at great expense.

Allen was a good kid. He was a spiritual leader and an active Christian. The first couple of years that he was in my youth ministry, he was a servant who had proper motives. When no one else wanted to get up early, he was at the prayer meetings. When everyone wanted to go home to sleep after an all-night event, he was willing to stay and clean up. He seemed to be on the right path. But something began to change.

His group of friends became closer. As they did, he became more distant.

Although his friends were all churchgoing Christians, they carried with them a pride that kept them from really pursuing God or working to serve others. They were often apathetic and complacent.

Allen's early teenage years were filled with positive growth, but when he hooked up with this particular group of friends, the growth came to a screeching halt. Instead of pursuing God, Allen would get caught up in just hanging out. Instead of praying for positive changes in their church, their youth group, their community, and their friends' lives, Allen and his friends would get together and critically find fault with others.

The misplaced priority of friends led Allen to an attitude of arrogance that isolated him from what God wanted to do in him and through him.

KNOW YOUR COMPETITION

Let's face the facts. Many teenagers struggle to keep their relationships in proper priority. The never-ending pull to have an active social life has dramatically affected many people's spiritual lives. Some relationships will have a negative impact on your spiritual life, while others will have positive results. If you allow yourself to be honest about where your relationships are, you might recognize some problems.

We have a strong tendency to defend our decisions in this area of our lives. Many teenagers justify unhealthy patterns, rationalize wrong priorities, and resist counsel from God and their parents simply because they think they know better. However, if you want to make sure that you do not trip on this obstacle, you must fight the urge to hide and defend. You must let God direct you into positive relationships.

People give many excuses for refusing to make the hard decisions when it comes to relationships. Here are a few of those excuses and why they should not be used.

"My friends need a positive influence, and if I stop hanging out with them, they are going to go downhill." Although

we do need to be good influences on those around us, we cannot let our attempts to save the world put us in danger. Many Christian students claim that they have befriended certain people to be an influence on them; however, because they are not strong enough, the Christians are the ones who are being influenced. Although God will ask you to get out of your comfort zone, he will not ask you to continually put yourself into situations where you are unable to stand. If you find yourself slipping in your convictions, it's time to make some changes. You can be selfish in this situation in order to protect yourself.

"I'm strong enough to stand." I can't tell you how many times I have heard a teenager say that he or she is able to stand against the pressure. He may use that excuse when he finds himself going to parties where temptation abounds. She may use it when she is in a dating relationship with someone who is putting pressure on her sexually. God asks us to stand strong when times are difficult, but he never asks us to *stay* in harm's way. Over the course of time, the same students who said they were strong ended up slipping in their convictions. Anyone who hangs around sinful influences long enough will become enticed. You might be stronger than most, but don't try to prove it by taking a chance.

"If I cut off my relationships with them, then I won't have any friends." I have come to believe that people who are truly serving God may have fewer friends, but they will be better friends. Rather than assemble a large group of acquaintances who will hold you back, you would be wise to find one or two friends who will help you become stronger than you currently are. The truth is that to protect your spiritual life you may have to make some unpopular decisions—but isn't it worth it? With a little patience and prayer, you will

discover that God brings you friends who are good to you and beneficial for your life as a whole.

LEARN GOD'S APPROACH

The Bible makes it clear that relationships enhance the quality of life. When you have quality friends around you, you have protection and strength.

> Two are better than one, because they have a good return for their work: If one falls down, his friend can help him up. But pity the man who falls and has no one to help him up!
>
> Ecclesiastes 4:9–10

However, it is also clear that by choosing poorly, you can put yourself at risk.

> Do not be misled: "Bad company corrupts good character."
>
> 1 Corinthians 15:33

Notice that the verse boldly states that bad company affects who you are. You simply cannot continually hang around people who have weak convictions and are living life selfishly and not be affected. They will have some effect on you on an unseen level. You will become weaker in your convictions if you are constantly influenced by those who do not share them.

TAKE THE CHALLENGE

To live a healthy life, you need to have a support group of good friends around you. However, you must avoid the danger of letting these friendships become more important to you than your spiritual life.

Keeping your social life in proper priority with your spiritual life is a difficult task, but one that needs your attention. If you neglect to evaluate your relationships, they may have a huge negative impact on your life. This is not something that you want to risk.

To approach this area of your life in a practical way, you must first evaluate it openly and honestly. Here are a few questions that you can use to take an inventory of the balance between your social and spiritual relationships and evaluate the direction in which you are headed.

Do your closest friends have the same spiritual goals? If your closest relationships are not with people who have the same mind-set and share the same goals, you will find it harder to reach your goals. However, if you have relationships with people who do share the goals of knowing Christ and becoming more like him, your objective will be much easier to reach.

Are you able to share your spiritual lives with one another and pray together? Sometimes the best way to work through your questions and fears is to talk through them with your peers. By surrounding yourself with people you feel comfortable sharing those parts of your life with, you are setting yourself up for radical growth. By praying together, you invite God to be a part of the relationship.

Do you influence your friends, or do they influence you? This is not simply a question of what kinds of things you do when you are together, but also of what kinds of attitudes, perspectives, and commitments you share. People who spend time together will begin to share outlooks on life. Usually the influence will be one way—one person will influence the other without also being influenced. If you are being influenced in a negative way, you may need to change your relationships.

Do your friends help you avoid temptation, or do they put you in harm's way? Your friends should not put you in situations where you are tempted to sin. Your closest peers should protect you from the things that are waging war against your soul and fighting to control you, not make your fight harder.

Are you pleased with your testimony when you are with them? In other words, do you like the person that you are when you are with these people? More importantly, is God pleased with you when you are with them? Do your times with them make you feel guilty, or are you satisfied with the decisions that you make and the way that you represent Christ? The answer to these questions should be soberly considered because next to your salvation, your testimony is the most important thing you possess.

Do you spend so much time on your relationships with your friends that you have no time left to invest in your relationship with Christ? This question more than any other will help you determine whether or not your priorities are out of line in the area of relationships. If you continually neglect spending time with God because your time is consumed by other relationships, something is out of balance. God never intended for you to have earthly relationships that are more important than your relationship with him.

Do your parents approve? I know that you don't want to hear this. Many teenagers think that their parents' opinions about their friends are crazy. But the truth is that parents have an intuition and a perspective that most teenagers do not. Parents see the subtle changes in their children when new relationships are being formed. Some of these changes are good and some of them are bad. If you refuse to listen to your parents' opinions, you are walking in dangerous territory. You are wise to ask for their counsel and heed their advice.

OVERCOME THE OBSTACLES

Mindy was athletic, relatively popular, and attractive. She had all the temptations that teenagers have, but she decided to seek God first and make him her number one priority. Rather than just say "yes" to any attractive guy that asked her out, she chose to evaluate each one's character and spiritual life before getting involved in a relationship.

Although this was not the most popular thing to do, it was the wisest. She had only a few close friends, but they were good ones. They supported each other and prayed together. Their spiritual lives benefited from the camaraderie that they developed.

She sometimes dealt with loneliness, but she didn't let it get the best of her. She learned to rely on God, who was always there with her.

Although she longed to be married, she did not rush into anything and waited patiently for God to bring her the right person.

Mindy is now married. She and her husband have a great relationship and can share everything together. As a couple they pursue God and serve him. Mindy was always content, but now she is overjoyed with the blessings that God has brought to her. She kept her priorities straight, and God honored that.

Mike had to make a tough call. After spending a couple of months investing in some relationships to influence some non-Christians, he realized that he was the one who was changing. His resolve was weakening. He recognized that he was going to begin having problems standing for Christ if his friends kept dragging him to movies, parties, and places that were not appropriate for a young man of God. He knew that he had to stop hanging out with them.

Rather than make a big production about it and make them feel like they were being judged, Mike simply stopped going out with them. He found a new set of friends and spent all his time with them. When his old friends called and asked him to come hang out, he said "no." However, he would turn the invitation around and ask if they wanted to come hang out with his Christian friends and do other activities instead. Some declined, but one agreed and is becoming friends with more Christians. After a few short months of observing that Mike took his faith seriously, this friend had been influenced so much that he was even willing to come to church. Mike protected himself from sin, but was still used by God to bring someone back to real faith in Christ.

Just like Mindy and Mike, if you keep your priorities straight, you can continue to grow with God and be a positive influence on those around you. But if your priorities get out of order, your relationship with God will suffer and your testimony will not be healthy.

PERSONAL GAME PLAN

Ask Yourself This—Who do you spend the majority of your time with? Like it or not, they are influencing you in some way. In light of your spiritual goals, are they good for you? Do you believe that God is asking you to make some changes?

Key Scripture—"Do not be misled: 'Bad company corrupts good character.'" 1 Corinthians 15:33

Ask God to Help—Surrender your relationships to the Lord by praying, "*God, I give you permission to speak to me about all of my relationships. I ask you to bring me friends who will be good for me. Give me wisdom and discernment with all of my friends so that I will not make unwise choices. Forgive me for the times that I have been influenced in negative ways by other people, and help me to live by my convictions. I ask these things in Jesus' name. Amen.*"

5

in the safe zone

Julie came down the stairs as her father arrived home from work. After a hug and a greeting, he asked where she was going. Her tone changed and she became defensive. "Out," she said.

When her father wanted more information, she refused to give it. Instead of working through the conversation, she stormed past her dad and slammed the door.

That night she went many places and spent time with many people. She did things and consumed substances that were neither legal nor wise.

Although this young woman had grown up in a Christian home and at one time had strong convictions, she had forgotten about them. Her attitudes about sex had begun to become less moral as she had entered high school. So had her philosophies about drugs and alcohol. Those changes took place as she entered into relationships with people who were not good for her. Because she was a follower, she began to go places that offered dangerous temptations. This mixture of people and unprotected places led her into a dark hole that will take months of struggle to escape. Even when she does finally get freedom from the habits, she will still have to deal with the ongoing consequences.

Kate always had a good head on her shoulders. She was an above average student who had a heart for the Lord. Although some of the young ladies in my youth group obviously struggled with the dynamics of purity in relationships, she was not one of them. At a young age she made a commitment to be sexually pure. And she successfully kept her vow—that is, until Brian came along.

She met him through a friend, and although he was not a Christian, she decided to begin a dating relationship with him. At first she kept her boundaries drawn firmly. However, after a short time, she started to give in.

As her youth pastor, I could tell that something was changing. She had been very active in church. She attended everything. However, after a few months of dating Brian, she stopped coming around as much.

I became nervous for her and tried to find out what was going on. I picked her and a friend up after school one day to go to a restaurant to talk. "Are you doing OK?" I asked. She quickly told me that she was. I asked, "Are you guys staying out of trouble?" Again, she told me that she was. She said, "Sean, I told God that I would not give up my virginity, and I meant it." After several minutes of talking, I warned her that sin has steps. Her goal shouldn't be to avoid only sex, but to avoid the things that lead in that general direction. She seemed to listen intently, but my heart told me that I was wasting my breath. She wasn't able to really hear my counsel because Brian was drawing her in.

About five months after that conversation, I listened to Kate tell me the terrible news that she was going to be having a baby. I say it was terrible news not because of my disappointment in her, but because of her disappointment in herself. She was so saddened by her mistake that she has been working to overcome those feelings for several years. I also say it was terrible news because it has affected her life in ways she was not prepared for. Although she has a beautiful child, she still had to deal with the emotions and struggles of being a teenage parent.

Kate herself will tell you that she made several mistakes. Although she trusted Brian at the time, she now realizes that he was only trying to use her. Because she did not take the proper precautions to guard her purity, she had to walk through some difficult trials.

Jason grew up as a moral teenager in a Christian home. Even though all of his friends began drinking alcohol every weekend, he said he would never start drinking.

However, as he began to hang out at the parties, the temptation became too much to handle. The first several times that people offered him a drink, he said "no." But after watching everyone around him drink and wondering what they were going to think of him if he didn't, he decided that one beer would protect his reputation.

The problem was, one was not enough. One beer at a time, Jason got hooked. As he became a regular at the parties, he became a regular at the keg.

Before long, he was offered stiffer drinks. He refused the first several times. He was content with his beer. However, his resolve weakened with each beer, and before long he was sampling other beverages.

The same scenario played out with the drugs. He refused to take a hit when they were passing around the joint, but he could only resist for so long. After a while, he was the one bringing the stash.

"Just marijuana, nothing else." That's what he said when people offered him heroin for the first time. But just like in the past, he eventually gave in.

By his senior year, this teenager with a Christian heritage was doing everything high. Very rarely was he sober. He struggled to even get out of bed without some substance in his body.

Jason lived this life for over two years before it all began to fall apart. On a break from college, he went home to party with his friends. On his way home he got pulled over. When the police officer looked in his car, he saw some drug paraphernalia and arrested Jason.

One year out of high school and Jason found himself in jail. Sitting in that cell, he began to evaluate how he had gotten there. Little by little his convictions had dwindled. It all began when he started going to the parties. He never meant to develop a drinking problem or start some addictions. He was just going to enhance his social life and have some fun. But in the name of fun, he put himself in a dangerous place. He was confident in his ability to stand, but his weaknesses were exposed.

After one night in detention, he was released. Walking out of the jail, he was met by his father and a camera. His dad was snapping pictures of him leaving that day because he wanted Jason to remember this experience. "Well, did you like it in there?" his dad asked. Jason could honestly answer, "No!" He did not want to spend another day in jail. The consequences of his mistakes were pretty minimal, but they could have been much worse.

In the couple of years since then, Jason has avoided jail and the problems that got him there. Shortly after his wake-up experience, he rededicated his life to Christ. Now he is aggressively pursuing God and doing everything he can to show the love of Christ to everyone he meets on his college campus.

Sam and Max were brothers who developed a gift for getting in trouble. Many times it could be traced back to their poor choice in companions.

One day I received a call from their parents saying that they needed to talk with me. A couple of days later the five of us sat down in my office. They shared their story with me.

"We got arrested the other day," Sam started. On Thursday they were hanging out with some of their friends at lunchtime. They were in the cafeteria eating and goofing around. One of their friends said that he was going to leave school and play hooky for the last part of the day.

Max jumped right on that. "Can I come?" Of course his friend was trying to recruit other people, so he was more than willing to bring Max along.

Knowing that Max was taking a chance on getting in trouble, Sam tried to talk his brother into staying at school. But instead, Sam got talked into leaving too. The pressure he felt from these friends was too much. He didn't know how to say "no." He wasn't willing to risk the torture of being the outcast or being teased for his lack of adventure.

Within minutes they were in a car driving down some back roads. But when they parked outside the house of a fellow student, Sam and Max knew they were in trouble. The driver of the car had a grudge against a student who had stolen his girlfriend, and he decided to make a statement while the other guy was in school.

Although the brothers were nervous, they followed their friend into the house through the open back door. Not knowing what he was planning on doing but too afraid to ask, they blindly walked into trouble.

Their friend disappeared upstairs as soon as they entered the house. After only three or four minutes he came downstairs with a few things in his hands and told Sam and Max to follow him.

They got in the car and drove off. As the driver talked excitedly about "showing him," the two brothers remained silent. Their nervous energy and lack of ability to stand up for what they believed made them seem proud of what they had just participated in.

That all changed when the lights of a police car appeared behind them. An aware neighbor had tipped off the police, and they had no trouble finding the three students.

At the police station, the driver blamed the brothers for everything and tried to pin the crime on Sam and Max.

As I talked with the family on that day, the sons voiced their disgust with themselves. In hindsight they could not believe that they had been a part of something so foolish. Their problem began when they chose to put more confidence in a friend than in their own beliefs.

I have seen this repeated so many times in the lives of teenagers. They are so eager to make friends that they will go along with anything, no matter how unreasonable. However, history has also proven that many times those who are so good at winning over other people will prove to be miserable friends in the end. They will often manipulate others while promising faithful friendship, only to disappear the moment that things get tough.

KNOW YOUR COMPETITION

Although damaged lives are horrible to see, I see it every week. In the fifteen years I have been working with teenagers, I have seen hundreds affected by poor decisions. Unwise choices in the areas of who they spend time with and where they go with them have taken many into dangerous areas and brought extreme consequences. Many lives have been ruined and many others hindered with excessive baggage.

The stories retold in this chapter are of young people who were raised in Christian homes. Although passion for Christ may not have been their number one priority, they each did have a foundation in Christian faith. They all had to deal with some very difficult things, but some of them did return to their roots in the faith.

These young people all possess one other similarity: They all thought it couldn't happen to them. A slight arrogance paved the way for their mistakes by keeping them from listening to the warnings of the people around them. Rather than pay attention when their pastor talked about ways to avoid the pitfalls, they tuned out. Instead of listening to their parents, they hid. If they had a book like this before they found themselves in trouble, they would not have heeded its warning; they might have skimmed it, but once they figured out the topic, they probably would have disregarded it altogether.

Please don't be like them. Learn from the mistakes of others, and protect yourself from their blunders.

LEARN GOD'S APPROACH

God's approach to these issues is often ignored by our society. He teaches an avoidance technique for dangerous situations.

> Flee the evil desires of youth, and pursue righteousness, faith, love and peace, along with those who call on the Lord out of a pure heart.
>
> 2 Timothy 2:22

> Avoid every kind of evil.
>
> 1 Thessalonians 5:22

Never once does God imply that we should exert our strength and prove that we can stand up strong if we have a way to avoid the temptation. He does not endorse the idea that perhaps we should put ourselves in a vulnerable situation just to enhance our social standing. He commands us to "flee" and "avoid" all of the evil that we can.

Another important thing to note on this subject is what God says about obeying your parents:

> Children, obey your parents in everything, for this pleases the Lord.
>
> Colossians 3:20

Teenagers often argue that parents don't understand or trust them enough. However, God commands us to obey our parents in "everything," not just the things on which we agree with them. Even if your parents' demands seem irrational to you, you must obey them. If you refuse and rebel, then you are disobeying God as well. You might not like your curfew or the restrictions they put on you regarding where you can and can't go and who you can go with, but you will be protected both spiritually and physically when you choose to submit to them.

TAKE THE CHALLENGE

Whether you are willing to admit it or not, the people you spend time with and the places you go will be either spiritually beneficial or morally challenging.

Although no young person wants to hear that the friends that they have are influencing them in a negative way and that they should consider making a change, the truth is that many students stumble because of the people they choose to spend time with. Likewise, no one wants to hear that they "should not" or "can not" go to certain places. However, if you do not make wise choices in this area, you will face some repercussions.

By taking the necessary precautions and being willing to make difficult decisions in the areas of "where" and "with whom," you can help protect yourself from destructive behaviors that might be waiting just around the corner. Here are a few practical questions to ask yourself.

What are the moral convictions of the people I spend most of my time with? Those closest to you will begin to influence the way that you think. If you spend lots of time with people who are always talking about sexual things, then your standards will begin to reflect that. You probably will notice the change first in your speech. If you are continually around people who are drinking and doing drugs, then your convictions on those activities most likely will begin to change. You can protect yourself from the kind of problems that have been discussed in this chapter by choosing wise friends who will encourage you to have high moral standards. But if you stay in the midst of low standards most of the time, you put yourself at risk.

Do the places that I choose to go put me in the path of temptation? I don't deny that temptation is everywhere, but you should do what you can to protect yourself. Instead of going to the parties where you will be continually tested, go somewhere safer. Working to avoid the places of greatest temptation may not make you the most popular, but it will help you avoid sin. Isn't that the goal?

Do I listen to my parents? Whenever I talk to teenagers about their parents and imply that students should listen to what parents say, I am looked at like I don't understand the culture. Students aren't expected to respect their parents. However, you can be protected by listening to them. They have a keen discernment about people that you sometimes do not have. Many times they can see the warning signs when you are spending too much time at one place or with specific people. If you listen to them, you can protect yourself.

Am I playing too close to the fire? Many people try to beat the system. "I can handle the party; I just won't drink." "I can hang out with these people; I just won't do what they do." "I know his reputation, but I can date him and remain pure." The problem is that we try to get close to the fire of temptation without getting burned. I propose that we should try it another way. Let's not get near the fire. The world throws enough pressure at us. We don't need to help.

Are my warning indicators still working? If so, do I listen? The Holy Spirit will try to warn you when you are starting to get into danger. However, many people have been ignoring these warnings for so long that they can't hear them anymore. Perhaps you need to invite God to let the alarm go off. And when you hear it, take the necessary precautions to get away from temptation.

Are there any immediate changes that need to be made? Dangerous places and the wrong people will eventually get you in trouble. Are there any areas in which you are either entering into sin or leaving yourself unprotected? I believe that God might be trying to speak to you about some specific areas. Are you willing to make the necessary changes? Although making the decisions that might make you unpopular is never easy, it is sometimes necessary. God wants to help you avoid the stumbling blocks that have been tripping up Christians for decades, but if you are not willing to make the changes, the warnings will not help you.

OVERCOME THE OBSTACLES

When your parents ask, "Where are you going and who is going to be there?" it is not an intrusion, it is a protective instinct. They realize you will be making decisions which may be influenced by your friends and the atmosphere of the location. They not only deserve answers to their questions about your activities, but they also deserve to have some input.

If you really recognize that the places you go and the people you surround yourself with will affect the majority of the things in your life, then you might be willing to think through your rights and choices. If you continue to deny that these things impact you, you may wake up one morning with regrets that could have been avoided.

PERSONAL GAME PLAN

Ask Yourself This—When was the last time that you found yourself in a dangerous situation that caught you off guard? Could you have avoided it by being more alert to your friends and your surroundings? Many Christian young people find themselves in danger because of who they hang out with and where they spend their time. Are you committed to avoiding stumbling over these obstacles?

Key Scripture—"Blessed is the man who does not walk in the counsel of the wicked or stand in the way of sinners or sit in the seat of mockers. But his delight is in the law of the LORD, and on his law he meditates day and night." Psalm 1:1–2

Ask God to Help—Pray about your relationships and temptations. *"God, my relationship with you is more important than my social standing. Because of that, I am willing to avoid any place that you want me to avoid. I will also listen to you for guidance for who I spend time with. Help me to choose wisely. Help me to listen to my parents. Even though these decisions are difficult, I thank you that you will reward me for making the tough calls. Like everything in my life, these decisions are yours. I love you. Amen."*

6

avoiding the pitfalls

Vince found out that moving into a new town can be hard for a teenager. His move brought a new school and a new environment and left behind his established friends. To top it all off, he had moved in the middle of the school year. Everyone immediately recognized him as being new.

When you are the new kid, one of your first desires is to fit in. That didn't come easily for Vince. His loud approach to life brought instant ridicule from the people in his new school. Within days he was being teased, pushed, and challenged. People were not only unfriendly, some were downright rude.

After two weeks of walking through the halls alone and eating all by himself, he was fed up. He embraced a group of friends who were rebellious and rough. Although Vince had never before taken to such people, his need for some companionship became too strong.

After Vince chose his new crew, he did notice three or four really kind people in his classes. After some discussions, he realized that they were Christians. One Friday they asked if he wanted to go bowling with them. He declined because he already had plans with his buddies.

As he walked away from the Christians to join the others, he had regrets. He knew that he had chosen friends that were going to end up leading him in dangerous directions, but his course was set. Two weeks was too long to wait to find good friends, so he had settled for the ones that he now had.

Kansas was a great girl who had tried to live uprightly through her teen years. However, her convictions began to slip slowly away as she became discouraged with her social life. She had been patient, but was finding it harder and harder to wait as she became more aware of her haunting loneliness.

Months passed as she tried to fight off her intense feelings, but she was fighting a losing battle. She needed someone—anyone—to ease her pain.

And there he was. He went to her church, but he wasn't the most respectable Christian. He had a reputation as a "player," but she didn't care. Her loneliness had made her need for companionship so strong that when he asked her out, she accepted.

Only two weeks into the relationship, she began to sense some problems. He was moving way too fast physically, but she didn't know how to tell him to slow down without risking making him mad and watching him walk away from the relationship. Because she would do anything to hold onto the only escape that she had from her loneliness, she let him lead her places physically that she had never been and had determined she would never go.

He only stayed with her for a total of eight weeks. He used her and moved on to another victim. For him it was just his typical pattern, but for her it was more painful than anything she had ever known. Her loneliness convinced her to put aside her convictions, and she is still paying for it. Before the relationship she was all alone, but now the added guilt of her sin, disappointment of losing him, and pain of being used have made her a sad and depressed young lady. She is a shell of herself, and all because her loneliness pushed her into places that she didn't want to go.

Kelli had always been a true friend to them. That is why she could not understand why her friends turned on her so quickly.

This group of girls had been tight since seventh grade. Because they were strong Christians, they never went the way of the crowd and always relied on each other. They had gone to dozens of sleepovers and watched hundreds of movies together and shared their lives in every way. The four were inseparable all through middle school and through the first years of high school—but suddenly things changed.

As Heather, Heidi, and Beth entered their junior year, they embraced a new goal. They wanted to fit in with the popular crowd. They wanted to climb the social ladder and gain the acceptance of the elite. However, this recognition came with a high price. They had to join in the snobbery of putting down others who didn't fit the right profile. One of the people they routinely mocked, teased, and discussed was Kelli.

Suddenly Kelli was not only excluded from their activities but also expelled from the circle of her old friends. She is still the sweet, kind, and godly young woman she always was. The change came in her friends.

Now Kelli is all alone and Heather, Heidi, and Beth are living a lie. They don't like who they are, but they are so caught up in their own pretense that they don't realize how they have changed.

KNOW YOUR COMPETITION

One of the main things that makes people stumble and lose focus in their pursuit of spiritual goals is the wrong way in which they pursue relationships. By failing to be wise in the area of their social lives, they stumble and sometimes fall. Not all relationships that are available to you will prove to be beneficial. You are going to have to make some tough decisions if you are truly going to be successful walking through these minefields.

If you are willing to wait for the right friends, they will benefit your life in many areas. However, if you act impatiently and choose the wrong friends because they are the most convenient, they will prove to be a stumbling block in your path. You must be determined to be patient about developing friendships. Otherwise you'll discover firsthand that impatience will lead to regrets.

Don't let loneliness dictate your social decisions either. Loneliness is a dangerous tool that the devil uses against people of all ages. He may even use it as he tries to make *you* stumble. Like a waterskier who is dragged wherever the tow rope leads, you can be dragged by loneliness into the dangerous areas of ill-advised relationships and inappropriate actions. And, like the skier, the person who is being controlled believes that he is in control of his destiny and can stay afloat in his attempts to master his social domain—but before he knows what happened, he may find that he has fallen and is in desperate need of someone's help.

Finally, make a decision *not* to participate in the petty games that so often rule relationships. Whether a group of girls decides to alienate a former friend or a group of guys exaggerates stories to impress each other, these games are built around shallow attitudes and selfish manipulations.

I am even seeing petty games at work with my daughters, whom I believed to be too young to learn or be affected by these games. My first-grader, Miranda, came home recently with a sad look on her face that worried me. I sat down on the chair next to her and hoisted her into my lap, and she laid her head against my chest for comfort. I asked her to tell me what was wrong. With the quiet voice that she gets when she is sad, she told me how her friend Claire had rallied her friends against her. Miranda had been playing on the monkey bars with several other friends when Claire wanted to show her dominance. She called over all of the girls except Miranda to play on the swings. For some reason, the girls who had been enjoying Miranda's company chose to go with Claire. They left behind a sad and hurt six-year-old. I have seen petty games happen in schools, colleges, and churches all across the country, but I never thought that they started this early.

Rather than play hurtful games, make a point of being an ambassador of love and friendship to those who might be left out, ridiculed, or picked on by the crowds. Don't side with the Claires of the world. And if you have already been hurt, don't look for your opportunity to get back at them. These games do not have a healthy origin, purpose, or result. Take a stand against them and for those who have been wounded.

LEARN GOD'S APPROACH

Although the Bible indicates that friends are a good thing and add to a healthy life, it also warns of the dangers of choosing incorrect friends. God tells us that wisdom is needed when choosing companions.

A righteous man is cautious in friendship, but the way of the wicked leads them astray.

Proverbs 12:26

God also goes out of his way to offer his friendship. And God is not the typical companion who is with you only in the good seasons—he will stick with you through every season of your life, no matter how good or bad it is.

A man of many companions may come to ruin, but there is a friend who sticks closer than a brother.

Proverbs 18:24

To have a healthy social life, you must walk in proper relationship with the one who longs to be your best friend. As you grow more confident that God is on your side, you will have the strength to handle the lonely moments. You will have the ability to trust him and be patient as you wait for God to bring you peers that you can relate to and share your life with. And you won't feel the need to play the games because as you build your identity around your relationship with Christ, your character will be strong and your desire to be truthful and to be a strong support for your other friends will grow.

The key to a well-prioritized and stable social life is a healthy spiritual identity based around the one who gave all that he could to buy a relationship with you. Invest in this relationship, and it will pay off in the other areas as well.

Greater love has no one than this, that he lay down his life for his friends.

John 15:13

TAKE THE CHALLENGE

Friendships are a gift from God. Pure relationships are special and add joy to life. However, unwise relationships can make you stumble. Here are some guidelines to apply to your relationships both for your protection and so that you can benefit everyone that you have influence over.

Make sure that your spiritual life is always more important than your social life. By making your decisions from a spiritual standpoint, you might not enhance your social life, but you won't allow it to destroy you either.

Quality of friendships is more important than quantity. You may have many acquaintances, but not many great friends. Don't entrust yourself to everyone, but only to those you know will build you up and not tear you down.

Don't sell out. God has great relationships in store for you, but you must have the integrity and conviction to not settle for something that is less than you deserve.

Don't manipulate with physical flirtations. Just because you are attractive and can get the attention of the opposite sex doesn't mean that you should. Rather than attracting attention with your looks, body, or flirtatious ways, strive to present yourself with modesty and godliness. Although it is not the way of the world, it is the only way you will develop good, lasting, and healthy relationships.

Don't forget about everyone and everything when you find a special friend. Many people make the mistake of forgetting about all of their other friends and all of their other passions when someone new comes along. Fight to include others in your circle rather than exclude them.

Don't isolate yourself from society because you found a new partnership.

Don't measure your self-esteem by how full your social calendar is. You are special, precious, priceless, and valuable—not because you are the most liked person in your school, but because you are the most loved person in the universe. God does not value anyone more than you. Therefore do not allow the number of your friends or dating offers to make you feel bad about yourself or give you some inflated perception of yourself.

Be a leader. As a Christian you are called to live by your convictions, not by the whims of the people around you. Stand up for what is right; don't cave in to hold onto some friends who are not true friends anyway. Be a leader, and others will follow you.

OVERCOME THE OBSTACLES

The teenagers who make it through their early years with a healthy self-esteem that was not ruined by poor relationships are more ready to make an important contribution to God's plan than those who compromised in this area. Instead of being a typical teenager whose life is defined by relationships, strive to be an atypical student who lets your relationship with Christ define you.

I encourage you not only to avoid the games that plague your generation, but also to commit to being a good friend and strong support system to those around you who need solid relationships. As you set an example of what it means to be a true friend and a dynamic follower of Christ, you will be helping them to be more open to God and influencing them to offer true friendship to those around them as well.

PERSONAL GAME PLAN

Ask Yourself This—When was the last time that you experienced extreme loneliness? Have you ever been wounded by the relationship games that so many people play? Make a conscious decision to not play them yourself. Are you a leader in your relationships? Commit to setting a good example for others.

Key Scripture—"A righteous man is cautious in friendship, but the way of the wicked leads them astray." Proverbs 12:26

Ask God to Help—Take time to pray for this area of your life. *"Lord, help me to always set a godly example for the people that are around me. May I never compromise my beliefs in order to find or keep friends, and may I rely on you, Lord, more than any person. You are my best friend and you desire to meet every need I have. Teach me to trust you, rest in you, and cling to you. I love you and I thank you for loving me. Amen."*

part 3

image

—— 7

the right image

I was going to stand before a group of students and share a message with them in just over an hour. Although I had been praying about this speaking engagement, my attention had not been focused on it for the past couple of hours as my wife and I had dinner with some friends. When we left the restaurant I began to mentally prepare for the opportunity that was before me. As we got closer to the church, I grabbed Mary's hand and asked her to pray with me.

As I prayed out loud, I began to recognize some wrong motives in my heart. I noticed things in my heart that were selfish and shallow. My prayers began to change as I focused on getting my heart right.

After I was done praying, I began to confess to Mary what I had realized about myself. I had suddenly recognized that I was more concerned about what people thought of me than about being obedient to God. I wanted the senior pastor to notice my gifts and abilities and to respect me as much as I respected him. I wanted the youth pastor, who had never heard me preach before, to be impressed by my speaking ability. And I wanted the students in the youth group to accept me. I would never be directly disobedient to the Lord just to impress people, but I had found myself more concerned about what they would think of me than about the things that God wanted to do in their hearts.

I knew that my motivations had to change if I wanted to be effective in ministry. I realized that if I was motivated by trying to impress people, I might compromise what God would ask me to speak. Once I realized that my motives were wrong and my desires to impress these people were selfish, I was able to give those feelings to God and ask him to purify my motivation. Through prayer, I got past my insecurities about what people think for one evening, and I had the privilege of being used by God to speak his Word to that church. And, as God so often works, the people there accepted me with open arms and received what I had to say. From that night on, with God's help, I have tried to keep an eye on my desire for the approval of others.

KNOW YOUR COMPETITION

No doubt you have had somewhat similar feelings to the insecurities I faced that night. After many conversations with others and seeing many people desperately trying to impress others, I have come to believe that most people have felt the same way at some time in their lives. They may not have been trying to impress a pastor or win the approval of an audience, but in other ways many have been very conscious of what other people were thinking about them.

Although everyone deals with these feelings, problems arise when your image is your main concern. Here are some of the problems that come when you let your reputation become the main factor that determines your actions.

> *You will not be obedient when God asks you to do something that might be considered unpopular.* If you are only concerned about making a positive impression on people, your ability to take a stand for the Lord will be hindered.
>
> *You will always wear a mask.* If your main concern is what others will think of you, you will find yourself being fake and hiding the real you. So even if others do like you, will they even know the real you?

You will end up giving away your individuality. Your uniqueness makes you special. You were created to be different
from every other person. But if you are only trying to protect others' perception of you, you will be too intimidated
to demonstrate any uniqueness. You will be forced to
conform to what you think people want you to be.

*You will always be looking for signs of acceptance from the
people around you.* The never-ending cycle of analyzing
what others are thinking has begun. Rather than enjoy their
company, you will be watching every expression and listening to every word to find out how they feel about you. You
may often overanalyze and misinterpret their messages.

You will create tension in your relationships. Our obsession
with what others think is caused by fear, and fear produces
tension between people. By letting your image control you,
you are creating a life of unnecessary stress.

LEARN GOD'S APPROACH

The Bible teaches that you were created in God's image. You
were his idea. However, the devil has put together a strategy to
try to destroy your proper perspective on image and identity.
Although the devil is working hard to mangle your pure motives
and force you into being self-absorbed and obsessed with what
others think about you, God can give you a better perspective.

God knows who you are better than you do. He knows why
he created you and how much potential you have. Because of
him, you have a hope and a future. His power at work in you
will take you beyond anything that you can imagine. And his
love for you sets you apart as irreplaceable.

To be successful in life, you must develop a proper perspective
on your image. This lies in understanding three things:

1. You were created to be *in him* (1 Cor. 1:30; 2 Cor. 5:17; Eph. 2:6). As simple as it sounds, God wants you to be grounded in the fact that you are a child of God. Without this revelation as a foundation, you will struggle. We can have confidence in the fact that we are God's and that his love is stronger than any force on earth. Because of this, we can keep our hearts focused on Christ instead of on what others say or think about us.

2. As you walk with Christ, you are becoming more *like him* every day (2 Cor. 3:18; Phil. 1:6; 3:10; 1 John 4:17). Although you are not perfect, as you walk with Christ and submit to his power working within you, you are in the process of becoming more like Christ. Rather than strive to make the world notice you, seek to know Christ more, to become more like him, and to develop your identity around him. As Christ becomes more noticeable in your life, actions, and character, you will feel less pressure to perform acts that will draw attention to yourself. You will want Christ to be noticed instead of yourself. As John the Baptist said, "He must become greater; I must become less" (John 3:30). Don't be discouraged if you realize that you are not as close to being Christlike as you should be or want to be. Although you have a long way to go, God promises that one day you will be like him (1 John 3:2). This life is an opportunity to work on some rough edges and improve on some faults. We all have too many faults to iron out in our lifetimes, but when we see Jesus, the work will be done.

3. As you walk through this life, you have the privilege of working *for him* (2 Cor. 5:20; Eph. 2:10). You have been recruited by a legend. You have been hired by the best. God himself has chosen to use you as part of his plan. You have the opportunity to represent him in this world and point everyone to him. What a fantastic and encouraging

truth that proves your value and worth! If you understand this, you will find security in who you are and be able to have a healthy self-image.

Understanding that you are *in him*, are becoming *like him*, and get to work *for him* is glue that helps the proper perspective on image stick to your heart.

TAKE THE CHALLENGE

Although you might recognize the need to trust God with your image, you may also feel that it is a constant fight. Putting your desire to be respected, esteemed, and appreciated on hold is difficult. Something inside of each of us longs to be noticed. But when your actions are dominated by this longing, you need to change your conduct. Here are some suggestions for starting the process.

Ask for God's help through prayer. By confessing your image problems and asking for God's help, you are getting your soul ready to overcome these difficult struggles.

Fight the urge to draw attention to yourself. If you are always in the spotlight because you have a need to be noticed, take a step into the background. Don't allow yourself to fight for the attention when you recognize that it is feeding your selfish desire to be seen. Learn to be content in the background until you don't need to be noticed.

Remind yourself that your identity comes from your relationship with God. You are special not because of your beauty, personality, or abilities, but because God created you to be unique and for a specific purpose. Because you are a special part of his creation and he loves you, you have tremendous value. These things are true whether or not you are conscious of them. However, by reminding yourself regularly of these encouraging truths, you can move toward having a more healthy identity.

Read Scripture that reminds you to brag about God yet walk in humility. Regularly reading verses such as these will build your faith in God while helping you keep your image problem in check: Romans 12:3, 15:17; 1 Corinthians 1:31; Philippians 3:7–8; and 1 Peter 5:5.

Go out of your way to serve others. Because you will find it difficult to serve someone else while wrapped up in your own image, look for opportunities to serve. Serving helps take your focus off of your own struggle to create an identity.

OVERCOME THE OBSTACLES

God wants to be your identity, protect your reputation, and weave your image together with his purpose for your life so that you will ultimately fulfill your destiny. Whether or not you recognize it, God is by your side, working with you to achieve his plans through you. Let him take care of what other people think of you.

PERSONAL GAME PLAN

Ask Yourself This—Do you have a tendency to look for other people to accept you? Who are the people who you try to impress the most? How can you overcome these habits to live a healthier life?

Key Scripture—"It is because of him that you are in Christ Jesus, who has become for us wisdom from God—that is, our righteousness, holiness, and redemption. Therefore, as it is written: 'Let him who boasts boast in the Lord.'" 1 Corinthians 1:30–31

Ask God to Help — Pray that God would help you trust him with your identity. *"God, I thank you that I am made in your image for your purposes. I am not insignificant. I have a purpose and a destiny. Lord, help me to trust you with my image and identity. May I not be consumed with what others think about me, but may I begin to hear what you say about me. Help me sense your encouragement and affirmation. I love you. Thank you for loving me. Amen."*

8

the comparison trap

Steve? Why him? Why did I have to have him in my class? And sitting right next to me at that.

On my first day of high school, third hour, I somehow ended up in a class with all upperclassmen. And not just any juniors and seniors. No, I ended up with the ones who ruled the school—the guys who brought out every insecurity I had buried inside of me and the girls who intimidated me with their looks and poise. Whenever I was around these people, I was extremely aware of how small, geeky, and insignificant I felt. Nothing I said seemed to come out right. Everything I wore seemed to point out my lack of both money and taste. Now I was going to have to spend a semester with the crowd who made me want to run and hide. And not only did I have to be in class with those who were higher up on the food chain, I had to sit right next to the one that was their leader.

Steve's reputation preceded him—I knew who he was long before I had any interaction with him. My insecurities and his image combined in my mind to make him seem like the most important guy in our high school society. He was the guy that every guy wanted to be like and every girl wanted to date. He was on the top rung in our school and he knew it.

In sports, he was all world. As a sophomore quarterback he had led our football team to the state championship game. His statistics for that game were beyond impressive. He carried the team and almost won the game by himself. Although they were huge underdogs, he led them to within two inches of the win. The replay actually showed that he did get into the end-zone on the last play, but the referee's call mattered more. The controversy only added to his air of mystery.

All the girls were impressed with him. When they saw him they would either flirt or melt on the floor in front of him. He was the man on campus as far as they were concerned.

He drove one of the nicest cars in the school parking lot and seemed to have plenty of money to do whatever he wanted.

When it came to attitude, he was bigger than life. He knew we all thought he was something special and he played it up. He walked with a little hitch in his step just to make him unique. Everything he did, he did with style and personality.

I am telling you, Steve was the king of our school, and I was sitting right next to him. I got more and more anxious as I tried not to reveal my immaturity in front of him, because I knew that if I did, he would point it out to everyone in the class, and I would be left without an ounce of dignity as everyone got a good laugh at my expense.

I was afraid of him yet wanted to be just like him. I wished that I could be as athletic as he was. I wanted his car. I wanted all the girls to want to be with me like they did him. I even tried to imitate his strut. But I became painfully aware that he would always be who he was, and I was stuck with me.

KNOW YOUR COMPETITION

Disappointed in who they are, many students wish that they could live someone else's life. Admiration is one thing, but wanting to trade your own life for another's is dangerous.

By comparing themselves with others, many students initiate a cycle that only makes them unhappier. Instead of finding a sense of comfort and peace in the fact that they are uniquely made with God's plan for their life in mind, they become more and more discontent with themselves. Their insecurities rage as they remind themselves how they lag behind others in certain areas and abilities.

Is this a problem? Is this dangerous?

It most certainly is. Your thoughts and perspectives can feed the emotional turmoil you are already feeling as a teenager. The more you compare yourself to others, the more you are adding to the confusion instead of working to overcome your insecurities.

If you are not content and you are continually longing to be like someone else, you will face many consequences. You will wear emotional masks to try to make yourself look better. You will play petty status games—which don't impress God—to try to gain the approval of the people you are trying to impress. You will avoid offering your uniqueness to the world because you fear that you won't be accepted because of it. All in all, you will become a poor imitation of the people that you are trying to be like instead of living like the unique creation that you are.

LEARN GOD'S APPROACH

I am convinced that one of the top priorities that God has for each of us is that we would be content to be the people that God made us to be. He created us uniquely and specifically because he knew what our world needed. He refused to create carbon copies—so why should we try to become them?

Although the enemy of our soul would love to convince us otherwise, when God designed us, he was intentional. We were not mistakes, and we were not random choices. Everything that we are came from God's conscious thought and perfect plan.

For you created my inmost being; you knit me together in my mother's womb. I praise you because I am fearfully and wonderfully made; your works are wonderful, I know that full well. My frame was not hidden from you when I was made in the secret place. When I was woven together in the depths of the earth, your eyes saw my unformed body. All the days ordained for me were written in your book before one of them came to be.

Psalm 139:13–16

Before I formed you in the womb I knew you, before you were born I set you apart; I appointed you as a prophet to the nations.

Jeremiah 1:5

God had a strategy when he was creating you. Before you were born, he knew where you would live and what you would be doing. He knew the influence that he wanted to give you, and he sculpted you to be effective at that task he had planned for you.

If you learn to be content with how God made you and thankful for the unique parts of your life, you will be much closer to both happiness and effectiveness.

Take The Challenge

I can easily tell you that you should be content and shouldn't strive to be someone else, but I know it is hard to do. Here are a few practical things you can do to move in that direction.

Be thankful for your uniqueness. Our society makes fun of the areas in which we are different. But wouldn't it be a boring life if everyone were identical? Instead of hiding the areas that make you different, learn to thank God for them. As you pray, list the things that give you a distinct and special approach to life. This might be a struggle for you at first, but as you fight through your insecurities and truly learn to appreciate these areas, you will be able to embrace them, even with other people. If you continue to look at these things as a curse instead of a blessing, you will hide them. In doing so, you will hide a large part of yourself.

Don't let negative comments come out of your mouth. Many people who feel awkward and insecure tend to put themselves down as a way of dealing with those emotions. They say negative things because they assume that other people are thinking them. I am convinced that this is one of the most dangerous things you can do. Rather than learning to embrace who God made you to be, you are insulting the unique characteristics that God built into you. If you are going to learn to be content in who God made you, you must put a stop to the self-defacing comments that come out of your mouth. Ask God to put a guard on your lips, and ask your friends to help you recognize when you make negative self-statements. You can stop these comments that wage war against your self-worth if you make it a goal. With the help of God and your friends, you can overcome this destructive habit.

Read Scripture that reinforces God's love for you. Our society works hard to convince us that if we don't look right, talk right, have the right material things, or excel at the right activities, we are not loveable. However, God disagrees. He loves us no matter what. If you are going to learn to be content with who you are, you must change the way that you think. Instead of embracing the world's view of significance, you must accept God's.

For this change to take place in your mind, you must begin to dwell on what Christ says about you through Scripture. If you read the Bible with your heart open to God's affirmation, you will find many places where he expresses his love for you. He applauds his creation — which you are part of — and loves it all for its uniqueness and specific calling. By dwelling on God's Word, you will begin to combat the lies that have been preached to you by the world. You might want to write down some verses and post them in places where you can see them every day—on the bathroom mirror, in your car, in your locker at school—so they become a part of who you are and how you think about yourself. Here are a few Scriptures to start with: Psalm 17:8; Psalm 139:13–16; Jeremiah 1:5; 29:11; Zechariah 2:8.

Choose substance over style. One of the main reasons that people are not content with themselves is that they are impressed by external qualities in others. They continually want to look as good as others seem. But the real goal should be to build character, not just popularity—to value substance over style. God is not impressed with appearance or personality, and we should not be either. We must fight to make our value systems match up with God's. It starts with being conscious of our tendencies to be drawn to external things when we should really be attracted to internal substance.

OVERCOME THE OBSTACLES

I very rarely meet a teenager who is content with who he or she is. I am convinced that even Steve, the king of my high school, had insecurities and at times was afraid to be himself. No one is perfect in this area; everyone cares what others think to some degree.

However, if we realize our tendencies, we can overcome them. We can move toward healthy views of ourselves and others. And if we are going to be all that God wants us to be, we must.

PERSONAL GAME PLAN

Ask Yourself This—Do certain people make you more self-conscious than others? Do you tend to sacrifice your uniqueness when you are with them because you are afraid they won't accept you? In what ways? Do you continually put yourself down? Describe the way you want the people in your high school to remember you.

Key Scripture—"For you created my inmost being; you knit me together in my mother's womb. I praise you because I am fearfully and wonderfully made; your works are wonderful, I know that full well. My frame was not hidden from you when I was made in the secret place. When I was woven together in the depths of the earth, your eyes saw my unformed body. All the days ordained for me were written in your book before one of them came to be." Psalm 139:13–16

Ask God to Help—*"Lord, I know that you made me special, and I thank you for that. You know I sometimes struggle to accept myself because I am afraid that other people won't accept me. I have a tendency to hide how you made me, but I don't want to. Lord, I need your help. Teach me to be thankful. Help me control my negative comments and thoughts. And help me stop comparing myself with others. I want to be a person of substance, not just style. Change my heart so I can live out what you want for me. Thank you, Lord. In the great name of Jesus I pray. Amen."*

9

behind the facade

Jim entered our discipleship school with an impressive résumé of Christianity. He seemed to have perfect credentials from being involved in many visible and prominent activities. He had good recommendations from every spiritual leader in his past. He came across as a hard worker, a devoted servant, and a humble leader.

However, sometimes things are not as they seem. Within a few months I began to see that his perfect spirituality was all a facade.

Jim's spiritual clichés started sounding more and more hollow as each week passed. Some of his actions seemed manipulative. And instead of being encouraging, his spiritual challenges had a condescending tone. Something was wrong, but we could not put a finger on it.

Finally we figured it out. Jim was masquerading as an on-fire Christian, but in reality, his faith had been dry for years while his mask had lived on. He had been playing spiritual games to win the respect and admiration of peers and leaders, yet all his spiritual activity was laced with pride and wrong motives. As we began to realize that he was wearing a disguise, he began to get uncomfortable. He began to pull away and hide even more.

Rather than stick around to let God use our school to challenge him out of his complacency, revitalize his faith, and test his character, he chose to escape with as much of his facade left as possible. He left our school halfway through the year to go home to the people who were still impressed by his spirituality. But soon even those people had figured out his game.

> Within one year of moving home, he had to move one more time. To keep his games working, he had to play them on new people.

KNOW YOUR COMPETITION

Wherever you go, you can see people hiding behind masks. Many people make creating an identity and sustaining a reputation a top priority. Unfortunately, what they work so long to construct is often nothing more than a facade, a false front. Sometimes the masquerade is so cleverly camouflaged that they even begin to believe their own stories.

The key to preventing yourself from getting caught up in your own deception is to recognize what areas, activities, and foundations you are building your reputation upon. Some are obstacles to creating an identity, while others will prove to be the proper outlets of time and energy.

I hope as you evaluate your life you will be able to recognize some positive trends and address some negative behaviors. To help you evaluate the areas where you might be hiding who you really are, let's look at some unhealthy things that people tend to build their images around.

> *Image-building through relationships.* I hate to admit it, but I was guilty of this one. In high school I felt like everybody thought I was a little odd. I saw my chance to change their impression of me when I got close enough to one of the popular girls to consider dating her. Although I did like her and enjoyed being around her, in the back of my mind I knew that certain people in the school would be impressed if we started dating. I was so surprised when she seemed to like me too. Sure enough, we started dating, and I temporarily improved my standing in the school.

Although people do use relationships to change the way others think about them, it is selfish behavior that shows shallow character. Finding a trophy date or snuggling up to the right people for your own advantage is not the right place to invest your time and energy as you are seeking to define your image.

Image-building through improved popularity. You have probably seen movies about teenagers who have tried to climb the social ladder by becoming popular. In these movies the students have been willing to leave behind their lifelong friendships, personal convictions, and distinctive personalities—all for one chance to change their status. They thought that if they could gain the overwhelming approval of the right crowd, happiness would follow.

In this case Hollywood has done a good job of representing a common theme found in real life. Most of those movies showed that in the end the shallow attempts to build an identity around improved social standing blew up in the person's face, leaving behind misery and wounded relationships as the truth was discovered.

The idea that "you have to be popular to be happy" has been forced on your generation. But it is a lie. Working so hard to build on such a poor foundation will only prove to be unfulfilling and destructive. Even if you can successfully get to the top of the heap, you will have to continue to wear the mask and play the games that got you there.

Image-building by relying on abilities. He was more than confident. He was downright arrogant. Everyone had told him how great he was, and it had gone to his head. When he walked into a room, he would draw as much attention to himself as he could. He had created an image for himself based on the things that he excelled at. This led to pride, and he ended up becoming frustrated when others started to out-perform him.

Although talent is "God-given," it is not how God defines you or how he wants you to define yourself.

Image-building by relying on appearance. She was definitely one of the most attractive girls in my youth group, but something about her was not right. I can still remember the first night that she walked in. Every male in the room noticed her. She was beautiful, but as we began to see her on a regular basis, we became less impressed.

Although she had all the right clothes and never went anywhere without doing her hair and makeup, her beauty couldn't hide the fact that she was rude and treated people with contempt. Her reputation in our group began to suffer. She seemed to forget that being attractive is about a complete package. Without an attractive personality, the Barbie looks quickly fade.

As you know, being attractive is not a sin, but it can become a curse. Relying on appearance instead of inward qualities to produce an identity might work for a short time, but in the long run, what is on the inside must enhance the exterior.

Image-building by relying on intelligence. Some people make a point of letting everyone know what they know. They get impatient when they have to explain something that they understand so well to someone who is less educated. This is another dangerous way to build an identity.

Although wisdom and understanding are worthy pursuits, making them the core of your identity is dangerous and unbalanced. Rather than laboring to impress people with the information that you have memorized, use your wisdom to help them. This will help you build your identity on who you are, not just what you know.

Image-building by flaunting your material goods. In this life some people are blessed with more material things than others. Some people try to make their things their defining factor, whether by the car they drive, the house they live in, the toys they have acquired, or the clothes in their closet. This approach to life is superficial and wrong. Gathering and flaunting things to make others think better of you is not a healthy way to define yourself.

Some Christians believe that living a materially blessed life is ungodly. Although I do not believe that to be true, I am convinced that those who spend their lives acquiring things in order to impress others are unbalanced and lack depth.

LEARN GOD'S APPROACH

The main reason that people feel the need to wear masks is that they are ashamed of the truth. They may be trying to escape the reality of the present, ashamed of their past, or have no hope for the future. When one of these three scenarios is true, wearing a mask may seem easier than dealing with their true emotions.

Yet God declares that we are a work in progress. In Christ the sins of our past have been forgiven, our present has been redeemed, and our future is promising. Because of Christ, we do not have to hide or pretend. No matter the shape of your past or the condition of your present, you can be content knowing that God is working on you and has your future in his hands.

TAKE THE CHALLENGE

Now that you have had a chance to evaluate some of the unhealthy things you may be trying to build your identity around, here are a few ways to move closer to a healthy identity.

Work on your spiritual life. God wants you to be defined by your love and pursuit of him. God desires that when people look at you, you are almost invisible because *he* receives the attention. If you want to develop into this kind of believer, you must invest in your spiritual life. Faithfully spending quiet time with God will help you change more into his image, and you will become known for your relationship with Christ.

Focus on improving your character flaws. Rather than trying to polish your mask so that you are able to hide your flaws and draw attention to your strengths, work to improve your inner character. You are well aware of your weaknesses and the areas in your life in which you struggle. If you ignore those things, they will continue to pop up at all of the wrong moments. But if you attack them through prayer, account-ability, and hard work, you will be tackling areas that truly are important and developing a stronger character.

Combat your image problems in prayer. You can take on your image problems directly by recognizing them and asking God to help you improve your motives. God loves to hear us recognize and confess the areas in which we have wrong motives. When we continue to pretend that everything in our life is in proper perspective and balance, we do not let God work in our lives. However, if we do an honest inventory of our motives and are willing to admit our weaknesses, he is able to help us overcome them. In prayer, tell God the ways you struggle with image. He is faithful to work in you.

Share your faith with someone. How can sharing your faith help you deal with your image? By making you take your eyes off of yourself and focus on someone else's needs. If you can take your eyes off of the mirror and look at the world around you, you will be less obsessed with your own petty problems.

Look for ways to serve others. At the heart of image problems is the tendency to be overly self-absorbed. Doing something nice for someone else requires a heart for someone other than yourself. Keep your eyes open for ways to do something selfless that will build up someone else's self-esteem. You could do something as simple as writing someone a note of encouragement. You could buy a small gift, compliment someone, or go out of your way to help someone. You will not only begin to overcome your own image problems, but also have a positive influence on how others view themselves.

OVERCOME THE OBSTACLES

Some people live their whole lives selfishly trying to impress the people around them. Rather than living for years handicapped by a need to amaze others, break the mold and demolish the facade at an early age. Invest in the areas that will make you who you want to be, and avoid the areas that will take away your pure motives and proper perspectives on life.

Although most people wear a mask at some stage in their life, you can get past the facade. With intentional effort and God's help, you can live openly and honestly as you let God take care of your reputation and image.

PERSONAL GAME PLAN

Ask Yourself This—Have you lost sight of what is really important because you have lived behind a well-designed mask? Have you tried to build your image around the wrong things? Wouldn't you like to live your life as one who is truthful and confident in who you are, rather than pretending to be someone that you are not?

Key Scripture — "You know my folly, O God; my guilt is not hidden from you." Psalm 69:5

Ask God to Help — *"God, I know that you value truth. You always speak the truth, and you reward those who walk truthfully. Please forgive me for the times when I hide who I am and wear a disguise. Help me to accept who I am so that I can let you help me overcome my weaknesses. I trust my reputation to you, for you are good and you love me, believe the best about me, and will continue to work with me until I become everything that I can be. May you be glorified in everything that I do and everything that I am. Amen."*

emotions

10

no more shame

Chrissy was obviously upset. In all the years that I had known her, I had never seen her cry. I was surprised to see her finding it difficult to hide her emotions that Sunday morning. When she saw me, she headed straight for me and asked, "Can we talk?"

Chrissy was one of the sweetest girls I had ever known. Although I would never claim that she was perfect, she was very innocent. At fifteen years old she had never been in any real trouble or tried to be rebellious. However, a few days before our conversation she had made some of the biggest mistakes of her young life, and she had to deal with some of the most extreme consequences.

My wife and I listened as Chrissy told us about her day at school on Friday. She got caught up talking to her friends after lunch and showed up to her next class late. That was one too many tardies, so after an hour in the principal's office, she was informed that she had been kicked off the track team.

A friend saw her moping through the halls and talked her into staying after school. In a moment of weakness and emotional confusion, Chrissy found herself out behind the school taking her first sips of alcohol. Because she was tiny and had no experience with drinking, she had very little tolerance. Within a few minutes she was feeling slightly buzzed.

Just then a teacher came around the corner and caught them. An hour later, Chrissy was sitting across from the principal with her mother sitting in the seat next to her. After announcing that Chrissy had been expelled from school, the principal confessed that he was disappointed in her. "Not as much as I am," declared her mother.

They sat in uncomfortable silence on the way home. Just before they pulled onto their street, Chrissy's mom spoke. "You know, I thought you were going to be different. But now you are just like everyone else. God is never going to be able to use you."

Although Chrissy had been able to hold back her tears as she told me most of her story, at this point she began to lose it. Through misty eyes she asked me, "Is it true? Will God ever be able to use me again?"

Although many things about the situation upset Chrissy, her mother's flippant comment was the most haunting. In one day she went from a "good girl" to a young lady with several mistakes to overcome. My wife and I reminded her of God's promise of forgiveness, but for months Chrissy would have to deal with the shame.

KNOW YOUR COMPETITION

As I look at our society, I see many people who are dramatically affected by shame. Shame is a sense of paralyzing guilt and disgrace that brings feelings of tension, insecurity, and humiliation. Its poison affects the lives of both teenagers and adults. It has no respect for age, race, religion, or wealth.

Even though most people either feel shame or have felt it in the past, many do not recognize or understand how it affects their lives. But those who know what shame looks like can pinpoint its activity and work to defeat it.

Where does shame come from? Shame often enters people's lives in one of these three ways:

> *Through sin and mistakes* — She lost her dignity when her actions were unveiled. She had suffered from guilt and shame as she kept her secrets hidden, but now that her sin had been exposed to the whole community, the intensity of those feelings was overwhelming.

Her story is told in John chapter 8. We do not know much about her distant past, but we know she had recently been in an immoral relationship. She had been caught in the bedroom of her lover and dragged into the temple courts for all to see. Her appearance might have given away what had happened, but the Pharisees made sure to describe her lifestyle—all her mistakes and failures—to everyone there.

To the religious leaders, she was just a pawn. They were using her to trap Jesus, and they didn't care what happened to her. But to Jesus, she mattered. Even as she stood there robbed of all self-esteem and rightfully condemned for her actions, Jesus reached out to her. Though she did not have enough confidence to even look him in the eye, Jesus defended her, gave her a new direction for her life, and began the process of removing her shame.

Just like the woman in this story, many people approach the Lord carrying the weight of shame because of their sins and mistakes. Although they may not have a crowd of people trying to remind them of their failures, their shame constantly repeats their shortcomings to them.

One of the reasons that Christ does not want us to walk in sin is that sin brings such harmful baggage and consequences with it. Although it is not often talked about, shame is one of the most devastating consequences of sin and mistakes.

Through pain and abuse—I wish the world was free from abuse, but it's not. Many, many people are walking around with shame that began when someone took advantage of them in some way.

In 2 Samuel 13, the Bible tells about a young woman named Tamar who was violated by her brother. Although both were children of David, Amnon was obsessed with his sister. He tricked her, cornered her, and forced himself upon her. She tried to fight him off physically and even tried to rationalize with him, but it was no use. Even as they struggled she recognized the shame that would come from this abuse, saying, "Where could I get rid of my disgrace?" (verse 13).

Her life was forever scarred. She was never able to get free from the memories that haunted her. The story ends by describing her as a "desolate woman" (verse 20).

High percentages of people in all walks of life and of all ages have experienced some form of abuse—sexual, physical, or emotional. Although the perpetrators are the ones who should be punished, many times the victims continue to suffer. Shame, dishonor, and disgrace try to attach themselves to the ones who have been wounded. If the victim does not fight off these emotions, he or she will struggle to experience the joy and peace of a shame-free life.

Because of a handicap—Acts 3 tells the story of a crippled man. Day after day, he begged for money—and also struggled to find acceptance and significance.

One day, he asked some of Jesus' disciples for money. He got much more instead. Recognizing that the crippled man was unwilling to make eye contact because of the shame of being different and standing out, Peter commanded the man, "Look at me." That day something perhaps more important than the strength in his legs began to be restored—his dignity.

Although most people are not physically handicapped, many people are held back in other ways. They walk around feeling that something is not right with them. They feel like they stand out and don't fit in. Some feel they are too tall, while others feel too short. Some feel guilty because they have a lot of money, while others fight to hide the fact that they don't live in the best neighborhoods and drive the nicest cars. Some people don't feel smart enough, while others are teased because school comes easy. Some struggle athletically, while some athletes struggle to live up to the pressure of others' expectations.

Whatever the cause, many feel that they have a handicap of some kind. That's when shame enters the scene. It reminds people of the ways they don't fit in and makes them feel more awkward. It makes them critical of their own features, quirks, and tendencies. These feelings result in a painful sense that they are lacking in something that they are supposed to be or have.

What does shame do to us? Here are five characteristics of people who are walking with shame in their life.

1. *They are handcuffed to the past.* Shame holds back people who want to step into a brighter future. Although most people want to move on from yesterday, many are held back by the regret in their lives. By keeping them tied to what happened in the past, shame keeps them from running ahead to something better.

2. *They have a negative view of themselves.* Like a monkey sitting on your shoulder whispering negative comments about everything you do, shame keeps you believing the worst about yourself. People who are dealing with shame struggle to see the growth in their lives. They fight an uphill battle to believe that they are valuable, gifted, and worthwhile. Shame is a constant reminder of the disgrace and dishonor of their lives. Instead of building a healthy perception of how God has made them and the miracles

that he is working in their lives, people who never learn to reject shame have a cynical view of themselves.

3. *They settle for less than they deserve.* In relationships, jobs, grades, and many other areas of their lives, people who walk with shame tend to settle for less than what they deserve. Shame persuades people to grab hold of the first thing that comes along. One of its most convincing lies is, "Be satisfied with this, because nothing better will come along." I notice this in relationships more than any other area. A beautiful, intelligent, godly young lady may choose to spend her affections on a young man that doesn't treat her right. Rather than wait for a good relationship, she settles for a bad one because she is afraid she won't find anything better.

4. *They get caught in the performance trap.* The performance trap has two extremes, and people who deal with shame might find themselves on either end of the spectrum. Sometimes they become perfectionists, trying to perform well enough to feel valuable despite their shame. At other times they will refuse to even try, feeling that they will never measure up to the expectations that have been set. The performance trap is a game you can never win. The perfectionist always sees his flaws and the things he can do better, while another person quits because he feels inadequate but only feels worse after giving up.

5. *They have no joy.* God wants joy to be one of the foundations of our Christian life, but shame can steal that joy. People carrying the emotional weight of shame find it hard to keep a proper perspective on God's work in the world. Instead of seeing their circumstances in light of God's power, love, strength, and gifts, they are overwhelmed with negative emotions. On the contrary, those who have overcome shame and gained a proper perspective will be

filled with a sense of wonder as they watch God work in their lives. Joy is a defining characteristic for people whose focus is on Christ and not on their own shame.

LEARN GOD'S APPROACH

If you too have been walking in shame, you need to begin to understand that God never intended for us to feel that way. When God created humans, they were without shame (Genesis 2:25). However, when sin entered the world through the disobedience of Adam and Eve, shame became one of the consequences.

As God looks down from heaven, he grieves when his children are hindered by shame. He sees how much pain it causes, and he wants to set us free. With God's help, you can walk free from shame!

The Bible has much to say about shame—the word is actually used in Scripture 128 times. In most of those references, God promises to help those who walk with him overcome the shame in their lives. Let's look at a couple of those references.

Anyone who trusts in him will never be put to shame.

Romans 10:11

Do not be afraid; you will not suffer shame. Do not fear disgrace; you will not be humiliated. You will forget the shame of your youth and remember no more the reproach of your widowhood.

Isaiah 54:4

Think about it: God promises that someday you will have forgotten the shame of your youth. The mistakes you have made, the abuses you have experienced, and the crippled feelings you have may haunt your thoughts today. But God can transform your life so completely that you will be able to forget those things. The intense feelings and overwhelming memories will one day fade.

> Instead of their shame my people will receive a double portion, and instead of disgrace they will rejoice in their inheritance; and so they will inherit a double portion in their land, and everlasting joy will be theirs.
>
> Isaiah 61:7

God desires to take away your shame and give you something better in its place that will bring you joy instead of disgrace. The good things that God has been storing up for you are not filled with memories of your failures. Instead, they are saturated with convincing evidence that he is a great God who is in your corner.

Take the Challenge

God will help you find freedom from shame. Here are a few practical tips that will be helpful for you as you choose to shake off shame.

Recognize that shame is not God's intention for you. At times you must choose to take aggressive action against shame through prayer. You will only be able to do this if you realize that shame is a curse from the enemy of your soul. Knowing that God desires better for you, you can confidently ask him to help you overcome your feelings.

Memorize Scripture that will help you stand against shame. Just as Jesus used Scripture passages to defeat the devil (Luke 4:1–15), you would be wise to have an arsenal of truth ready to fire off every time feelings of shame come to visit.

Change the way that you talk. Many people who are hampered by shame are very critical of themselves. They degrade themselves with the words that they use. If you have a tendency to do this, make a concentrated effort to change your speech patterns. You might be wise to tell your best friends about your decision to be more positive as well so that when they hear you tear yourself down, they can remind you not to participate in what shame is trying to do to you.

Receive God's forgiveness. If your shame comes from sin and mistakes in your past, accept forgiveness and don't let the devil bring it up again. If you are still participating in areas of sin you are ashamed of, work to change your ways, confess your sin to God, and begin to leave shame behind. No one can take away God's forgiveness.

Don't believe the lie that abuse was your fault. If your shame comes from abuse or abandonment, don't let shame tell you that it was your fault. That is never the case. Stop taking the blame for what an unhealthy person has done to damage you. Ask God to help you forgive them, stop dwelling on the memories, trust others again, and reject the shame.

Ask God to make you grateful for the things that make you unique. If you feel "handicapped" because you are different, don't let the things that make you special make you feel awkward. Ask God to remind you that he loves you just as you are and made you unique for a special purpose.

OVERCOME THE OBSTACLES

Shame is a destructive attack on your self-worth. If you let it, it will dominate your life, handcuff you to your past, and keep you from pursuing your destiny. Don't let it win in your life. With God's help you can walk free.

PERSONAL GAME PLAN

Ask Yourself This—Do you recognize the effects of shame in your life? Which of those listed most impact you? With God's help you can walk free from shame.

Key Scripture—"Do not be afraid; you will not suffer shame. Do not fear disgrace; you will not be humiliated. You will forget the shame of your youth and remember no more the reproach of your widowhood." Isaiah 54:4

Ask God to Help—If you realize that shame has been damaging your life, take time to pray. *"Lord, thank you that you love me and want me to walk free from shame. Please bring me to that place in my life where I no longer remember the shame of my youth. If my shame has come from my own sin and mistakes, please forgive me and give me the strength to overcome those areas of my life. If it comes from abuses or injustices that have been done to me, please protect me so that those things do not happen again and help me forgive those who took advantage of me. If it comes from feelings of awkwardness, give me a new level of confidence that comes only from you. God, I trust you to work these miracles in my life. I am yours and I love you. Amen."*

II

the battle against hopelessness

I can still remember the conversations that first night in the cabin. Since it was my first year at basketball camp, my teammates who had been there before decided that it was their job to inform me about what was ahead. For several minutes I lay in my bunk listening to their stories. Most of them centered on "D-Day." This was the day at camp set aside for testing your limits and pushing your body beyond what you thought you could endure. I drifted off to sleep wondering just how tough it could be.

D-Day for those in my age bracket was set for Thursday. As the day approached, even some of the veterans began to look worried. I actually saw fear in their eyes as they prepared for bed on Wednesday evening. Everyone in the cabin was abnormally quiet, as if they were preparing for what was ahead.

I went to bed that night wondering what I was going to experience the next day. Twenty-four hours later, my question had been answered, but I did not like what I had learned.

Thursday morning was announced by the ringing of the camp bell. Shortly after that, our coach was walking through the cabin to hurry us along. The urgency in his voice made us dress and prepare for the day quickly. After a quick breakfast, we were herded onto buses to take us off the grounds. The buses were too quiet. A silent fear dominated the atmosphere. After a short ride, we arrived at a local college campus. D-Day began the moment we walked off of the bus.

A man who looked like a military drill sergeant met us. He barked orders with the intensity and volume to match. As soon as we were lined up outside of the bus, he yelled, "I am going to push your body harder than it has ever been pushed. When this day is over, you are going to have fewer limits and fewer excuses. Today some of you are going to cry because your bodies hurt so much. Some of you are going to want to give up, but you will keep going."

Although we had never been formally introduced, I decided right away that I did not like this man.

He led us inside and gave us our first instructions for the day. "We are going to begin this day by doing one hour of wall sits."

Having played sports all of my young life, I knew what wall sits were, but I had never been asked to do them for one hour. A wall sit is the very painful exercise of "sitting" with your back against a wall and your legs at a 90-degree angle. With no chair to support your body, your legs and lower back begin to scream for you to stand up after just a few minutes.

After about thirty-five minutes, I looked over and saw the guy who played center on the team crying from the pain. He wanted to quit, but the rest of us on the team would not let him. If any one of us stood up before we were given permission, the whole team would be penalized with more time added to the clock. We were allowed a three-minute rest every fifteen minutes, but those small breaks did not make the task much easier.

For the first six hours of D-Day, I struggled and sweated through everything we were told to do. Our faces all showed our agony and most of my teammates had either cried or been on the verge of tears. At 3:00, I was the one crying.

I huddled in the corner during a short water break. My body was throbbing with pain. I was mentally ready to give up. I was hurting, overwhelmed, and hopeless. I didn't think that I would be able to go on.

Just as I was about to quit, the coach who had yelled at us as soon as we walked off of the bus invaded my space. With sensitivity in his formerly gruff voice, he said, "Don't give up. You can make it. There are only two hours left." Putting his arm around my hunched-over shoulders, he said, "I have been doing this for several years, and I have never had anyone die."

I looked up as he was walking away. But he was not finished encouraging me. He looked back at me one last time and smiled. I knew then that I could make it.

Without a full understanding of what I experienced that day (they made us promise we would never reveal all of the gory details), you might not think that was a whole lot of encouragement. But it was enough to change my perspective and convince me that I could handle the rest of the challenge. Here is why:

I was reminded that my challenge was only temporary. After the coach walked away, I glanced at the clock and knew that in two hours I was going to be back on the bus headed for the camp. I felt a new sense of determination knowing that I could handle anything, no matter how difficult, for a short amount of time.

I knew that the coach in charge knew what I could handle better than I did. This coach had been running hundreds of teenage athletes through the ritual that had affectionately become known as D-Day for years. After looking into his eyes and seeing that beneath his tough exterior he did have my best interests in mind, I began to trust him.

Although the last two hours were just as difficult as the first six, I had a sense of hope that I did not have before. As the clock approached 5:00, I found new momentum. Others were near total exhaustion, but because of my newly learned lessons, I was beginning to feel good about myself.

KNOW YOUR COMPETITION

Although you may never be put through the kind of painful experiences that I was that day, no doubt you can relate to the things that I was feeling. At one time or another each of us is put into a situation we feel we can't survive. Although we may never articulate our hopelessness, we all experience seasons of great difficulty in our lives. We may feel hopeless and fearful about the problems we face as we wonder if or when it will ever get better.

Just as I was pushed to the limits of my endurance, you may have been pushed to the point of wanting to quit trying. Maybe you have lost hope that your family situation will ever improve, so you have decided to distance yourself from your family for your own protection rather than to keep praying for God to work a miracle. Maybe you have been so overwhelmed with your own failures that you have stopped working to overcome them. However you can relate to hopelessness, I pray that you can draw strength and courage from the truths that are in these next few pages.

Hope is too precious to give up without a fight, because trust in God and hope in his unseen plan and power are what keep us moving forward.

Without hope you will experience worry, anxiety, and depression.

With hope you will have the ability to keep going, joy, and expectations for better things ahead.

As you can see, hope is a worthwhile pursuit!

LEARN GOD'S APPROACH

Here are some truths that will help you deal with feelings of hopelessness.

Even when you don't understand what is happening in your life, you can be sure that God does. Just as I took courage when I realized that the coach had been training athletes for a long time, you can feel good about the fact that God is aware of your situation. He is watching over you and will not let you be put into a situation that will destroy you.

This time of your life is not going to last forever. Although your feelings will tell you that things are never going to get better, the truth is that you will be through this sooner than you think. Chances are that in a short amount of time the struggles that are haunting you now will not be the main concerns of your life. Remember, you can endure anything for a short amount of time. So don't give up.

Hope is eternal, not just temporary. Even if your world falls apart, you can still have hope. Hope comes from having the perspective that eternal things are infinitely more important than the temporary things that happen in life. Even if your relationship with your family or closest friend is on shaky ground, God's love for you will never disappear. If you don't have enough money for a nice house or nice things, you can focus on the fact that in a short time you will be living in a heavenly mansion and walking on streets that are made of gold (Rev. 21:21). No matter what is happening to you now, if you are in Christ your future looks bright because your eternity is secure. When the temporary is over and eternity has begun, you will face no more difficulty, sadness, or hardships. Hope comes from this eternal perspective.

Hope comes from God's promises. If you keep your heart open to what God says about you and your life, you will begin to see things differently. You will begin to anticipate demonstrations of his goodness, grace, and love in ways that affect every area of your life.

I don't understand why people will so easily trust people who have a history of dishonesty or unreliability but not trust the one who has never lied or taken advantage of them. They believe someone who has treated them badly in the past has changed, only to be disappointed. At the same time, they will refuse to put their lives in God's hands—although he wants to protect them, guide them, and enhance their life in every way.

Do not fall into this trap if you want to make hope a reality in your life. God's promises should bring us hope, but we must choose to believe them.

God promises that he will not allow us to be crushed. First Corinthians 10:13 says that God will not let us be tempted beyond what we can bear. That word *tempted* means more than the pull of sin. It actually means that he will not let us face any situation or circumstance that will be too much for us. When you are going through a difficult time in your life, realize that God knows that you can handle it. Recognize that he has tested your character and determination and knows that you are capable of getting through the situation. And the more we invite God into our lives, the more we receive his help.

God promises that we can have peace. When people who don't know Christ talk about peace, they mean peaceful circumstances. When God promises peace (see Phil. 4:7), he is promising to provide peace even in chaotic situations.

He is the God of peace (Phil. 4:9), Jesus is the Prince of Peace (Isa. 9:6), and peace is a fruit of our lives as we walk with the Holy Spirit (Gal. 5:22). However, peace is not something we gain and then set on a shelf. It is constant evidence that God is working in our lives and giving us a calm assurance that he is in control and on our side.

Whenever you face something that tries to steal your hope, it is also waging war against the peace that God wants you to walk in. Hold onto peace; it is a part of your inheritance as a child of God. Jesus said, "I have told you these things, so that in me you may have peace. In this world you will have trouble. But take heart! I have overcome the world" (John 16:33). What a reason for hope!

God promises you that you are loved. Hopelessness often comes from strong feelings of being unloved and all alone. The world can seem unbearable when we feel that we have to face it all alone.

I am convinced that one of the reasons that Satan and our society work so hard to keep us feeling unloved and all alone is that it makes us easier to manipulate. When we are continually looking for someone or something to make us feel valuable, we are in danger of doing things that we are not proud of and do not want to do.

However, when we receive God's love willingly and freely, we have hope. Our convictions are stronger and we will run life's race well.

Most people have heard that God loves them (see John 3:16), but many struggle to believe it and therefore walk through life without hope.

TAKE THE CHALLENGE

When you find yourself dealing with real and overwhelming feelings of hopelessness, remember a few practical things that you can do.

Ask God for help. As always, you can take your problems to God in prayer. Although he already knows what you are feeling, you can weaken hopelessness' hold on you on some level by confessing your feelings. You will also be inviting God to work in your life.

Fight for hope by dwelling on positive things. By reminding yourself that God is on your side, that things will get better, and that your hopelessness is rooted in lies and emotions, you can start to overcome the paralyzing effects of hopelessness.

Read and memorize Scripture that reminds you of God's protection. King David wrote many psalms about the comfort and safety of being protected by God. You will discover that your faith in God will be strengthened and your panicking emotions will be calmed by reading those poems and prayers.

Don't give up. No matter what your emotions tell you, keep
fighting. God will not put you in situations that will crush
you. However, he will allow you to go through things that
will mold your character and fortify your faith.

OVERCOME THE OBSTACLES

If you want to live a productive, joyful, and fulfilled life, you
must hold onto hope. This will be a battle when the seasons
of your life turn difficult. In those moments you will have to
fight to keep your perspectives and attitudes right. Even when
the world around you tries to convince you that life is terrible,
believe God—who has an eternal perspective—more than you
believe those around you.

If you have been weary of fighting this fight and you have been
knocked down too many times by the world, you may need to
sneak a peek at the clock and remind yourself that this won't last
forever. And you would also be wise to find some time to pray
and remind yourself that God's in control.

PERSONAL GAME PLAN

Ask Yourself This—When was the last time you felt that things
would not or could not get better? When you feel this way,
what are some practical things that you can do to remind
yourself that God is still in control of your situation?

Key Scripture—"Never will I leave you; never will I forsake
you." Hebrews 13:5

Ask God to Help—In the moments when you feel hopeless,
realize that God can do miracles. Even when your situation

seems impossible, God can and will come through. Remind yourself of that by praying. *"Lord, you are always in control, and you never leave me on my own. Even though I cannot see you or feel you, I trust that you are working on my behalf. Lord, teach me to trust you and your faithfulness. Help me to fight off feelings of hopelessness as I learn to rely on the promises you have made to me. I pray these things in Jesus' name. Amen."*

12

overcoming insecurities

I spoke at a small youth camp in Michigan a few months ago. In one of the evening services, I encouraged the students to run to God to find out the truth about themselves. Using an analogy of a tent set aside to meet with God (Ex. 33:7–11), I taught them how to meet with God. At one point in my talk with them I said, "When the world tries to tell you that you have nothing to offer, pull out your tent and let God tell you what is true." The next day an extraordinary encounter happened.

A smug young man had approached a sweet young girl and tried to steal her self-esteem. He boldly told her, "You are ugly and fat."

Although most young ladies would have been either too embarrassed or too hurt to respond, she did something that totally surprised the rude eighth grader and everyone watching.

Reaching in her pocket, she pulled out her imaginary tent. She went through the motions of opening the tent and climbing inside and then got down on her knees. As about ten people watched, she closed her eyes and asked God a question out loud: "God, am I ugly?"

She waited a few seconds, smiled, and then got to her feet. Motioning like she was putting away her tent, she looked at the guy who had just insulted her and said, "God doesn't think I am ugly. He says that I am the crown of his creation."

Now the guy was the embarrassed one. He didn't know what to say, so he quickly turned around and left. Everyone else smiled as the young lady stood there with dignity and the one who had tried to embarrass her walked away.

KNOW YOUR COMPETITION

One of the greatest battles you will face in this life is the battle for your self-esteem. You will be tested and attacked from many different angles. Wrong messages will bombard your mind and heart. Some of these attacks will be verbal while some will be more subtle. Some will be vicious, outright attacks, as on the girl at camp, while some will come at you as the world's ignorant philosophies, subtly trying to point out how you don't measure up.

Although these attacks are real and will be difficult to deal with, they can be overcome. But first we must realize where they come from. Here are a few areas we can see the attacks.

False messages in the media. The media rarely shows us reality. Most of today's popular stars have been forced into the mold of what our society wants us to believe is the normal standard of attractiveness.

On one level we know those unnatural facades are not normal. Yet these false messages send real people into destructive spirals as they try to live up to these unrealistic standards.

Samantha's long red hair made her stand out in a crowd, and her warm personality was visible in her attractive smile. She was an attractive young lady whom everybody admired and believed to be beautiful. Everyone, that is, except herself. She didn't see what everyone else did. She had believed the lie that unless you have firm abs and toned muscles and weigh in at the perfect weight, you are abnormal. Her insecurities led to an eating disorder so that she could shed those extra pounds that only she saw.

Samantha bought into the lies that she saw on television and in the magazines. She allowed herself to be convinced that only people with perfect features could truly be worthwhile and happy. She never forced this opinion on anyone else, but she held herself to an unrealistic standard. Not only did she hurt her body pursuing this idealistic image, but she fell into many destructive behaviors and relationships trying to prove her value.

We must begin to recognize and deal with this great lie that the media has forced on our society.

Comparison with others. Nothing good ever comes when we begin to compare ourselves with someone else. When we do this we are looking to point out someone's faults—either our own or, if we believe that we are better, someone else's. Although it is hard not to compare, we must try. By comparing physical features, performance, abilities, intelligence, spirituality, or any other characteristics, we will inevitably hurt someone.

Jeff was very bright. He was always at the top of his academic class and also willing to give a helping hand to those who struggled in class. He regularly tutored athletes who struggled in math or science. However, Jeff was not happy. He had an overwhelming sense of insecurity in the area of sports. He hated gym class because of it. He couldn't catch a football. He couldn't make a basket. He struggled climbing the rope, and he was embarrassed whenever he had to lift weights. He compared himself physically with the jocks and didn't like what he saw. And his mind inflated the differences and told him that the athletes all were laughing at him behind his back.

Comparisons begin a vicious cycle. Although Jeff was a great guy with a caring personality, his insecurities about athletics drove him to withdraw and hide from people. Yet the same people that he did not measure up to athletically felt insecure around him when it came to academic things.

If you are going to walk free from insecurity, you must fight the urge to compare. Nothing good comes from it.

False value systems. We create false value systems by placing high priorities on things that are not supposed to dominate our desires. When we discover we can not achieve value based on these things, we are once again left with insecurity.

Steve always wanted to fit in with his high school crowd. He thought the one thing that could help him blend in was a nice car—but the ten-year-old station wagon he drove was an embarrassment to him. He noticed the nice cars his friends drove. The new truck, the well-cared-for muscle car, even the clean economy car seemed to shout curses at his station wagon. So when he arrived at school, drove up to the gas station, or showed up at church, he thought everyone was looking at him and laughing. His car was not helping him achieve the image that he was striving for. Rather, it was one of the main sources of his insecurity. Rather than find confidence in who he was, he let the car he drove steal his self-esteem.

Steve made the common mistake of thinking his value was tied up in his car. But many other false value systems are out there trying to coerce your generation into believing lies about your worth. Many people see themselves as either valuable or not because of their material things. Others believe their value is in their abilities or looks. Some believe it is in their intelligence.

The problem with these value systems is that they are based on false foundations. We are valuable because we are made in God's image. He loves us, his hand is upon us, and he paid a great price to purchase a relationship with us. Fight off the false value systems of the world.

Words that have wounded. Many people experience insecurities because of the careless words of others. Words flung about without much thought or meaning sometimes come to rest on people who have problems forgetting them. Most of us remember insults or negative comments much easier than we recall compliments. Many people in our society have painful insecurities because a parent, sibling, or friend made a comment that hurt them. They have kept it inside of them since the day it was made.

Standing in the youth room, I overheard a couple of girls talking about dating, marriage, and their desires to have God bring them godly men. Butting in, I found out that they were talking about how they were having a difficult time waiting. Looking directly at one of the young ladies, I made a flippant comment about how painful it was to watch her throw herself at every new guy who walked into the church. The comment, which was made in jest, was actually the opposite of what I thought about her. After a few minutes of laughing and joking with them, I walked away to have another conversation.

Several weeks later the girl made an appointment with me to ask if I had been serious. I was embarrassed to say that I didn't even remember what comment I had made. After she reminded me of my silly comment, I apologized many times over. In no way did I feel like she was a flirt, a player, or a manipulator. I respected her a great deal for her patience in waiting for God to take care of her needs. Here was a girl who had done everything right, but instead of making her feel like I was proud of her, I made a sarcastic comment which she embraced as truth. It hurt her and attacked her sense of security.

Many people have experienced the attacks that flippant words can bring. I often talk to teenagers who recall comments made by a mother or father, brother or sister, teacher, coach, or boss. Most of these words were not meant to wound them, but have done so nonetheless.

If some remarks weigh heavy on you, you probably need to deal with them. Whether that means going to the person who said those things or just giving them to God in prayer, do not let those words continue to gnaw on your self-esteem and eat away at your self-worth. If you recognize that your words may have hurt someone else, take it upon yourself to apologize and try to bring healing to the people you have hurt. Don't be someone who wounds others with words, and don't let someone's flippant or sarcastic attacks hinder you from being who God wants you to be.

Learn God's approach

The Bible makes it clear that God cares about people who are wounded. The insecurities that plague the human race are started by the enemy of our souls to keep us from seeing ourselves as valuable and loved by God. But God, the lover of our souls, longs for us to see ourselves from his perspective. His word is full of encouraging and positive statements and commitments to you. Here are just a few.

Zechariah 2:8 says that you are the "apple of his eye."

Zephaniah 3:17 says that God takes "great delight in you" and "rejoices over you with singing."

Song of Songs 8:7 describes the kind of love that he has for you by saying "rivers cannot wash it away."

In Jeremiah 29:11, God promises that he has good plans in store for you, plans which include "a hope and a future."

Psalm 139 says that you are precious to God and "fearfully and wonderfully made" (verse 14).

Many parts of Scripture talk about your value and worth to God. What he says about you is true. Your insecurities may seem to speak louder when you are saturating yourself with influences that preach lies. However, if you take time to learn what God says about you and meditate on those things, your insecurities won't stand a chance.

TAKE THE CHALLENGE

My dad once said to me, "Pick your battles well. Not all fights are worth fighting." That's good advice. People get caught up in battling many things that are not worth their time and attention. Rather than focusing on a good cause, they become distracted as they waste their time and energy on battles that are not worth fighting. However, fighting against your insecurities is a worthy cause.

If your insecurities dominate your life, you will always be wondering what others think of you, and you will never be comfortable and carefree in social settings. You will always walk in fear and feel the need to protect yourself from what makes you insecure. Insecurities do not produce anything positive in your

life. Take aggressive action against them! Here are a few suggestions to help you overcome them.

> *Dwell on messages of truth based on God's Word.* Your inse-
> curities will try to get you to see yourself in a selfish and
> isolated way based on who you are as a flawed human.
> Therefore the best way to combat insecurities is to dwell
> on what God says about you as a child of God whom he
> loves.
>
> Many places in the Bible, God tells you how much
> he cares for you and how he views you. By meditating on
> these statements and choosing to accept that they are true,
> you can wage war against the negative perceptions that are
> trying to steal your self-esteem.
>
> Review the list of Scriptures mentioned in the above
> section and continue to search for additional verses that
> reinforce God's view of you.
>
> *Learn to have proper perspectives on life.* Fight off false mes-
> sages, value systems, and comparisons by training yourself
> to have proper perspectives.
>
> I have been in full-time youth ministry for the past
> fifteen years. During that time I have asked God to give
> me an ability to tell when someone is using an excuse or
> flat-out lying to me. I can honestly say that I have a great
> ability to see lies coming from a mile away.
>
> When I see a young couple who have been dating for
> some time, something in my pastor's heart wants to know if
> they are avoiding the physical temptations that come with
> those kind of relationships. I often ask the question, "So,
> how are you doing?" The tone of my voice usually indicates
> that I am not simply asking, "How is your day going?"
> Rather, I am asking, "Are you staying out of trouble?" I

am not sure if it is because of their body language and unspoken signals or if it is because God's Spirit is speaking to me, but I can usually tell when they are lying to me. I feel almost like an alarm goes off in my head. When I hear the alarm, I always respond. Sometimes I will ask again, "You sure you are doing okay?" They may not change their story, but I will at least make a mental note, "That is not true. They are struggling."

Those conversations remind me not to believe everything that I hear. We need to have those same kind of conversations in our heads when our insecurities tell us to accept things that aren't true. When you feel unloved, it is okay to mentally remind yourself, "That is not true." When the subtle voice of the enemy whispers, "You are worthless. You can't do anything right," your heart and mind should shout, "That is a lie!"

By actively fighting every lie with a statement of truth, you will begin to easily recognize harmful thought patterns as they try to infiltrate your mind.

Remember that your insecurities are built around lies. Therefore you must recognize the lies and embrace the truth if you are going to win these fights.

Find contentment in who you are, recognizing that you are different than other people. We know that all people are different. Just as no two snowflakes are identical, no two people are exactly alike. We all have different personality traits, passions, perspectives, abilities, backgrounds, mental capacities, and physical features. Although we all recognize that we will never be like anyone else, we let those differences feed our insecurities.

Rather than getting upset because you can't throw the football the way the quarterback can, find your strengths and embrace them. Instead of beating yourself up because you aren't as creative and artistic as the person next to you in class, be content with the things that you are skilled at.

Learn to forgive the people who have hurt you, and try to walk in love and understanding. Many times our insecurities convince us to hold onto hurts and offenses. The people who played a part in creating our wounds are also handcuffed to the memory of our pain. When we hold onto these hurts and continue to hold others responsible, we cannot walk free and begin to be made whole again. Although letting go of offenses and dealing with the bitterness they bring will never be easy, it will always be one of the major steps to overcoming our insecurities.

Sherri had been in bondage to a poor self-perception all of her life. As I talked with her about the insecurities she was dealing with, we continued to come back to some issues with her dad and brother. Their rude and insensitive comments haunted her. The ones made around the adults and older teens who used to come over to their house to visit especially traumatized her. Their freely spoken comments embarrassed her so much that she withdrew. She chose to hide all of her feminine features. She wore baggy clothing that hung off her body. The hairstyle she chose was unflattering and tomboyish. She even consciously avoided activities that most girls enjoyed.

Sherri tried to fight through these issues for two years, but to no avail. She avoided discussing the hurts in her past, but when directly asked about them, she had a visibly hostile attitude toward her male family members.

One night at camp, after hearing a message on forgiveness, she made a conscious effort to forgive. She will tell you that it was not easy. However, knowing that God required it of her, she kept fighting to forgive.

Slowly her exterior softened. Her spiritual life began to move forward by leaps and bounds. As her heart toward her dad and brother began to change, her feelings toward God also began to improve.

Two years later, she is doing better. Although no one told her to, she let her hair grow out. Her clothing styles have started to change a little each season.

She worked hard to give up unforgiveness because God commanded it of her (Luke 6:37), and she found that when she did, her insecurities affected her less.

Most likely something has been done to you or said about you that the world would say gives you the right to hold a grudge. However, God does not give you that option. When you hold someone as a hostage of bitterness and unforgiveness, you will not only be directly disobeying God, but also find that you are embracing your insecurities.

OVERCOME THE OBSTACLES

God's whispers of love can become louder than the world's shouts that bring you down.

My wife recently gave birth to our first son. Some complications with the pregnancy led to him being delivered five weeks early. He was born on a Friday night, and on Saturday morning he taught me a valuable lesson.

Less than eight hours after the delivery, while my wife was asleep, I slipped out of the hospital room to go to the nursery for a little visit with my son. When I got there I found him bundled up and protected in his little blanket. I picked him up and held him close to my chest.

Because he was so premature, he was very tiny. After a few minutes of simply looking at him, I found myself leaning close to his ear and whispering, "You are perfect. You are beautiful." My encouraging words turned into prayers as I quietly asked God to watch over him, protect him, and shape him into a man of God. My first conversation with my son was a memorable one, but within a few minutes God used it to help me understand how he deals with his kids.

As I walked back to the room to see if Mary was awake, I felt God say to me, "See, that is how I treat you. When you are silent and take time to be alone with me, I will hold you in my arms, lean down, and whisper encouraging things into your heart. Although you can't understand them, you will begin to know that they are true."

If you, like so many people in the world today, deal with insecurities, take time to hear God whispering over you. The world is much louder, but God never lies. Our society will use every tactic that it can to convince you that you are worthless, unattractive, or hopeless, but God will speak truth to you. And if you take the time to let him speak to your heart, his whispers will be louder than the world's shouts.

PERSONAL GAME PLAN

Ask Yourself This—When do you recognize your own insecurities trying to dominate your attitudes? Can you pinpoint some areas where the attacks against your confidence are most noticeable? What can you do to fight against these things?

Key Scripture—"The LORD your God is with you, he is mighty to save. He will take great delight in you, he will quiet you with his love, he will rejoice over you with singing." Zephaniah 3:17

Ask God to Help—Attack your insecurities through prayer. *"Lord, you made me. I was formed in your image, and even though I am not perfect, you are continually working in my life to help me become who you want me to be. Forgive me for the times when I believe lies about myself. Forgive me for the times when I believe the influences of the world and the media instead of your Word. You are a great God and I am your child. Help me live with confidence and conviction. In Jesus' name, Amen."*

conclusion

let the competition begin!

I was fascinated. I don't remember how old I was when this new show premiered on Saturday afternoons; I just remember being glued to the set. Something about this intense (and somewhat illogical) competition had captivated me.

The show was called American Gladiators. The premise was to pit normal, everyday people against bodybuilder foes who were paid to punish them. Naturally, the overdeveloped warriors were referred to as the Gladiators. Each one had a name and a persona to intimidate those who would dare to challenge them. "The Enforcer," "Zeus," and "Goliath" were just a few of those who battled against the men, while "Storm," "Rage," and "Clash" waged war against the women. The Gladiators' tight spandex outfits were specifically designed to draw attention to all muscle groups and enhance the appearance of these Saturday afternoon mercenaries. The whole production was completed with cheering sections for each of the warriors.

The competition sometimes became very violent since the events were specifically designed to give the Gladiators an unfair advantage over their opponents. A flight attendant might find herself in a race to the top of the rock climbing wall with Storm on her heels trying to pull her off before she could ring the bell, while other shows depicted Zeus waiting expectantly to ambush a carpenter as he tried to successfully swing to the other side of the large auditorium on jungle ropes. Some events even had multiple Gladiators battling a single contestant.

As the show progressed you could see the bumps and bruises adding up on the contestants. Many times you would see someone lose sight of his goal of competing and simply try to protect himself from the attackers.

For some odd reason this show grabbed me and held my attention. I watched it whenever I could. But I didn't really know who to root for. Something inside of me wanted to cheer for the people who were just like me. Yet another part of me was behind the giants who were attacking them. Every time I watched, I was faced with this dilemma for the first forty-five minutes. However, the last part of the show was always the same, and it always got the same response.

The last competition was definitely my favorite. It was a kind of obstacle course, but it had one very unique characteristic: As the contestant strategically wound his way through the obstacles, he had to avoid the tennis ball missiles being shot at a dangerous velocity by an angry Gladiator.

At one end of the large auditorium stood an oversized bodybuilder who had spent months developing the skill to take down anything that moves with this large tennis ball gun. At the other end stood a normal person with the specific goal of making it to the other side as quickly as possible without being shot. Sometimes the cameras would capture the determined look in this person's eyes—other times it was a look of fear.

A gun would go off to start the clock running. The Gladiator began the war with the contestant as he began the trek through, around, and over the obstacles that stood in their way. The tennis balls flew by at intimidating speeds, but the determined players realized that they must stay aware of their enemy and focused on their goals.

Those who forgot about their nemesis would often have to leave the game early because a tennis ball had nailed them someplace on their body, leaving them trying to shake off the pain and deal with the embarrassment. Others made more progress. Sometimes with skill, other times with luck, the player would sneak from item to item continually dodging the incoming missiles.

Very few accomplished the goal of defeating the Gladiator, but I always hoped that it was their destiny. Those who did win earned a special kind of joy as they gained the respect of those they had fought against. They had stayed the course, remained focused on the goal, avoided the obstacles, and achieved success.

SO WHAT?

Even if you have never seen these Gladiators, you can learn from them. Just like them, you have both a goal and strong opposition. You have a destiny, but to get there you must overcome the odds, avoid the ambushes, and fight the good fight. God is in your corner and the crowds in heaven are pulling for you, but you must still do some things to be successful.

You must stay focused. To know Christ and become more like him is the only goal you should desire to build your life around. You must make achieving an intimate walk with him your definition of success and the foundation of your life. This goal must be your driving force. It must be the obsession of your days and your meditation as you drift off to sleep at night. You must stay focused on what truly matters. Anything else is the icing on the cake.

No matter what you achieve in life, if you aim for the wrong goals, you will be disappointed and unsuccessful in the long run. However, if you stay focused on the truly important goal, you will win.

You must protect yourself. Because you have an enemy who has spent centuries perfecting his weapons of destruction, you must be willing to protect yourself. Sometimes protecting yourself means doing the unpopular thing. Sometimes it even means doing something that you would rather not do. Rather than fight for your rights and defend your preferences, you would be wise to ask God for wisdom and direction so that you can walk closely with him. If you are willing to avoid some things, rearrange some priorities, and stop investing in some negative areas, then with God's help, you can walk victoriously.

Remember that missiles of devastation are flying at you on your journey of faith. You cannot afford to run aimlessly, nor should you try. But if you walk wisely, stay alert, and take the necessary precautions, you can make it out unharmed.

You must keep growing. God's desire for your life is that you continue to grow spiritually, becoming more in love with him and more like him every day. That is the challenge that lies before you.

I did not write this book to give you a list of rules for your life, but to expose the obstacles that might affect your growth. If all you get out of these pages is a checklist of things to avoid, you are no better off, because these lists will be a burden of religion rather than a measure of your relationship with Christ. If you do the right things for the right reasons—with a strategy and desire to grow in Christ—you will grow. But if you do the right things for the *wrong* reasons, you will become self-righteous and prideful, and you will definitely be no fun to be around.

You must keep growing. For these pages to have their full effect, you must combine the principles of avoidance with an attitude of pursuit—avoid negative things and pursue Christ, the one thing that should consume you. Do not be like so many Christians who get caught up trying to perfect their mask yet forget to really run after Christ. Although the contestants on *American Gladiators* would have found it easier to hide from the missiles until the clock ran out, they would not have found it as rewarding as striving for their goal.

THE CHANCE OF A LIFETIME

Watching *American Gladiators* was entertaining to me. The hour-long competition was intense, thrilling, and fun to watch, but something inside me wanted to play. I wanted to strap on my helmet and take on those spandex heroes. I wanted to run the gauntlet and defeat Goliath. I dreamed of the day when I might be able to climb the wall and ring the bell while fighting off the toughest of competitors.

Although I never got my chance to compete on this television show, I am involved in my own reality show. My walk with God is where I face my greatest challenges and overcome my greatest obstacles. Daily I fight to win the war against everything that would try to slow me down, get me off track, or destroy me. Weekly I face competition that, although unseen, is very intense and incredibly meaningful.

The consequences of failure are always on my mind, as are the rewards that await me if I stay on course. I must passionately live with eternity in mind, because the show doesn't end in an hour.

The same goes for you. You are in the midst of a serious competition, and God is in your cheering section. You can win. You can be victorious. With determination, you can endure and continue to compete.

The journey of faith is tough, but it is also full of joyful moments that make it well worth the difficult times. Don't let the obstacles trip you up. Don't let the barriers discourage you. The challenges are great, but the destination is worth it.

Now is the time to run toward your goal. Recognize the threats that lie before you and protect yourself, but get going. The path is narrow, but the reward is great. Strap on your helmet and get ready for the ride!

PERSONAL GAME PLAN

Ask Yourself This—What kind of person do you want to be in ten years? What do you want your spiritual life to look like?

What are the main obstacles that you are going to have to avoid in order to have a healthy walk with God? To thrive in your walk with God, you are going to have to stay focused, protect yourself, and keep growing. What actions can you take to guarantee spiritual growth in your life?

Key Scripture — "Like newborn babies, crave pure spiritual milk, so that by it you may grow up in your salvation, now that you have tasted that the Lord is good." 1 Peter 2:2–3

Ask God to Help — Let's close our journey together in prayer. *"God, thank you for your desire to help me grow in my faith. I want to be all that you want me to be. So once again, I commit myself to you. I lay myself in your hands and ask you to mold me and shape me. Help me to stay focused on you and to recognize the obstacles that will slow me down or knock me off track. I pray that I will continue to grow closer to you every moment of every day. I want to know you and serve you, for you are my passion. You are all I need. Continue to walk with me and work in me and through me. Be glorified in everything that I do, everything that I say, everything that I think, and all that I become. I am yours. Amen."*

Sean Dunn is founder and director of Champion Ministries, an outreach that introduces young people to living a life based on a relationship with Jesus Christ. He is the former youth director of a church in Castle Rock, Colorado, where he resides with his wife and four children.

For a free newsletter and a list of materials from Champion Ministries or for information on having Sean Dunn minister at your church, conference, retreat, camp, school, or other ministry group, please contact the ministry at:

Sean Dunn
c/o Champion Ministries
P.O. Box 1323
Castle Rock, CO 80104

Phone: 303-660-3582
E-mail: champion@championministries.org